Class,
Politics,
and the Individual

Class, Politics, and the Individual

A Study of the Major Works of D. H. Lawrence

Peter Scheckner

Rutherford • Madison • Teaneck
Fairleigh Dickinson University Press
London and Toronto: Associated University Presses

© 1985 by Associated University Presses, Inc.

Associated University Presses
440 Forsgate Drive
Cranbury, NJ 08512

Associated University Presses
25 Sicilian Avenue
London WC1A 2QH, England

Associated University Presses
2133 Royal Windsor Drive
Unit 1
Mississauga, Ontario
Canada L5J 1K5

Library of Congress Cataloging in Publication Data

Scheckner, Peter, 1943–
   Class, politics, and the individual.

   Bibliography: p.
   Includes index.
   1. Lawrence, D. H. (David Herbert), 1885–1930—
Political and social views.   2. Social classes in litera-
ture.   3. Politics in literature.   I. Title.
PR6023.A93Z8654   1985   823'.912   83-49456
ISBN 0-8386-3197-5

Printed in the United States of America

Contents

Acknowledgments	6
List of Abbreviated Titles	7
Introduction: Class Consciousness and Contradiction	9
1 Society and the Individual: *Sons and Lovers, The Rainbow,* and *Women in Love*	23
2 Class Conflict and Reaction: *A Collier's Friday Night, The Widowing of Mrs. Holroyd,* and *Touch and Go*	70
3 Revolution and Retreat: *Aaron's Rod, Kangaroo,* and *Plumed Serpent*	89
4 Radical Commitment to Eros: *The First Lady Chatterley, John Thomas and Lady Jane,* and *Lady Chatterley's Lover*	137
Bibliography	171
Index	174

Acknowledgments

I wish to thank Viking Penguin Press for permission to quote from Lawrence's published works. These include all the fiction and nonfiction works with the exception of *The Plumed Serpent*. For permission to quote from this novel I would like to thank Alfred A. Knopf Inc., copyright 1926, 1951. I am grateful in particular to Laurence Pollinger Ltd. for permission to quote from all the editions of Lawrence.

Of course we all share in a community of ideas and scholarship. If I have added at all to the vast field of Lawrence criticism, I would like to thank the following people in particular: Professor Richard Wasson of Rutgers University for his careful and dialectical reading of my work, and for his expert pedagogy; Professor Without Portfolio Charles Scheckner, for his humanism and enduring love of literature; Bella Shiffrin, Teacher Ecumenical, who showed unflagging enthusiasm; and for Pat Keeton, without whom this project would have been—at least at times—impossible.

Abbreviated Titles

A — *Apocalypse* (New York: Penguin, 1976).

AR — *Aaron's Rod* (New York: Grosset and Dunlap, 1922).

CL — *The Collected Letters of D. H. Lawrence,* ed. Harry T. Moore, 2 vols. (New York: Viking Press, 1962).

CP — *The Complete Poems of D. H. Lawrence,* ed. Vivian de Sola Pinto and F. Warren Roberts (New York: Viking Compass Edition, 1971).

CPL — *The Complete Plays of D. H. Lawrence* (New York: Viking Press, 1966).

CS — *The Complete Short Stories,* 3 vols. (New York: Viking Press, 1961).

FLC — *The First Lady Chatterley* (New York: Dial Press, 1944).

JT — *John Thomas and Lady Jane* (New York: Penguin Books, 1977).

K — *Kangaroo* (New York: Viking Press, 1960).

LCL — *Lady Chatterley's Lover* (New York: Bantam, 1968).

LG — *The Lost Girl* (New York: Viking Press, 1968).

M — *Movements in European History* (Oxford: Oxford University Press, 1971).

PF — *Psychoanalysis and the Unconscious* and *Fantasia of the Unconscious* (New York: Viking Press, 1960).

Ph 1 — *Phoenix: The Posthumous Papers of D. H. Lawrence, 1936,* ed. Edward D. McDonald (New York: Penguin, 1978).

Ph 2 — *Phoenix II: Uncollected, Unpublished and Other Prose Works by D. H. Lawrence* (New York: Penguin, 1978).

PS — *The Plumed Serpent* (New York: Vintage, 1951).

R — *The Rainbow* (New York: Viking Press, 1961).

S — *Studies in Classic American Literature* (New York: Viking Press, 1964).

SL — *Sons and Lovers* (New York: Viking Press, 1958).

WL — *Women in Love* (New York: Viking Press, 1960).

Introduction
Class Consciousness and Contradiction

Lawrence is the one major figure in modern British literature whose social background is working class. "I was born among the working classes," Lawrence wrote in his "Autobiographical Sketch," and "brought up among them. My father was a collier, and only a collier." Throughout his life Lawrence anguished over the fact that he could not sustain a deeper attachment to his father's people. He continually agonized that the British miner was either too hypnotized by materialism—the Mammon of property and money—or too dead in spirit to revitalize English society. Nevertheless, Lawrence identified deeply with this class, and workers appear in all his major works. In the "Autobiographical Sketch," completed in June 1928, the author concludes:

> I cannot make the transfer from my own class into the middle class. I cannot, for anything in the world, forfeit my passional consciousness and my old blood-affinity with my fellow-men and the animals and the land, for that other thin, spurious mental conceit which is all that is left of the mental consciousness once it has made itself exclusive. (*Ph 2*, 596)

In the same year, Lawrence wrote a collection of poems called *Pansies*. "The Saddest Day" described his climb up the social ladder:

> O I was born low and inferior
> but shining up beyond
> I saw the whole superior
> world shine like the promised land.
>
> So up I started climbing
> to join the folks on high,

9

> but when at last I got there
> I had to sit down and cry.
>
> For it wasn't a bit superior,
> it was only affected and mean;
> though the house had a fine interior
> and the people were never in.

The poem ends with this stanza:

> And so there came the saddest day
> When I had to tell myself plain:
> the upper classes are just a fraud,
> you'd better get down again.
>
> (Stanzas 2, 3, and 10)

Lawrence's class background and the rigid class structure of England had an enormous and lifelong influence on the author. Even while he argued in many of his works that "class makes a gulf, across which all the best human flow is lost" (*Ph 2*, 595), Lawrence painstakingly described the effects of class on men's lives.

By social class Lawrence meant a great deal more than one's relationship to the means of production or how much wealth or property one may have inherited. Lawrence ascribed economic, ideological, cultural, and psychological characteristics to class. He claimed that because workers were in direct and continual contact with machines, nature, and other men, they tended to be uncomplicated and direct among themselves; they experienced sex deeply and spontaneously. In *Rainbow,* for example, the Brangwen men on Marsh Farm manifest some of these class-defined qualities. The opening pages of this novel describe at length the "blood intimacy" that the Brangwen farmers feel between their lives and their work: "the body of the men were impregnated with the day, cattle and earth and vegetation and the sky (*R*, 2)." In *Sons and Lovers,* Lawrence's description of the collier Morel as "soft, non-intellectual, warm," is fairly characteristic of the miners in Lawrence's short stories. The typical worker in Lawrence's works is sociable, passionate, and uncomplicated. He has a potential for humaneness unmatched by the upper classes. Lawrence rarely suggested that the natural camaraderie of workers made them a revolutionary force—or even that such a force was necessary—but his understanding of social class did include various political, social, and psychological qualities.

Introduction

Many of the contradictions in Lawrence start with his conflicting view of class and class struggle. As aware as he was of the implications of class, Lawrence shied away from drawing the political conclusions his portrayal of workers might have suggested. He railed bitterly against the dead materialism of European politics and the destructiveness of class struggle, but he consistently showed how capitalism limited human development and killed human potential. Lawrence had few illusions that man was free of economic necessity, that he was independent of the restraints imposed by a class society. In an unusually long letter to his one-time friend Bertrand Russell, in February 1915, Lawrence raised the central questions that all his major works ask: To what extent can the individual be free from social responsibilities? Could a man find salvation in a woman's love before he dealt with the social question? How could man act to free himself from the economic question? Was purposeful social action possible? Could class struggle be the agent of change? These are then the issues that Lawrence developed in his novels, plays, and short stories.

Freedom in the abstract is an illusion; no man is naturally free from society, politics and economics. Lawrence described "the solid basis of freedom of actual living," that which could free man to explore his potential for creativity and love:

> There must be a revolution in the state. It shall begin by the nationalising of all industries and means of communication, and of the land—in one fell blow. Then a man shall have his wages whether he is sick or well or old—if anything prevents his working, he shall have his wages just the same. So we shall not live in fear of the wolf—no man amongst us, and no woman, shall have any fear of the wolf at the door, for all wolves are dead.[. . .]
> Something like this must be done. It is no use saying a man's soul should be free, if his boots hurt him so much he can't walk. All our ideals are cant and hypocrisy till we have burst the fetters of this money. Titan nailed on the rock of the modern industrial capitalistic system, declaring the fine language that his soul is free of the Oceanids that fly away on winds of aspiration, while the bird of carrion desire gluts at his liver, is too shameful. [. . .] So there must be an actual revolution, to set free our bodies. For there never was a free soul in a chained body. That is a lie. [. . .] The freedom of the soul within the denied body is a sheer conceit. (*CL*, 317)

A while later Lawrence wrote that he was essentially a radical. As a writer it was necessary to act against the whole framework of society:

12 CLASS, POLITICS, AND THE INDIVIDUAL

There comes a point when the shell, the form of life, is a prison to the life. Then the life must either concentrate on breaking the shell, or it must turn round, turn in upon itself. [. . .]

Now either we have to break the shell, the form, the whole frame, or we have got to turn to this inward activity of setting the house in order and drawing up a list before we die.

But we shall smash the frame. The land, the industries, the means of communication and the public amusements shall all be nationalised. Every man shall have his wage till the day of his death, whether he work or not, so long as he works when he is fit. Every woman shall have her wage till the day of her death, whether she work or not, so long as she works when she is fit—keeps her house or rears her children.

Then, and then only, shall we be able to *begin* living. Then we shall be able to *begin* to work. Then we can examine marriage and love and all. Till then, we are fast within the hard, unliving, impervious shell. (*CL,* 320)

He never entirely abandoned this point of view. As World War I dragged on, Lawrence became increasingly embittered against the British worker and the chances for social progress; yet he was pulled in two directions: he desired radical social change while fearing political militancy. Throughout 1915 he called for a social and political revolution in England, but in July of that year he worried that "the war is resolving itself into a war between Labour and Capital" (*CL,* 351). However, in a letter to Mary Cannan in February 1915, he spoke of the need for a social revolution:

Since I have been here, it has come upon me that we must have a social revolution, after the war. Private ownership of land and industries and means of commerce shall be abolished—then every child born into the world shall have food and clothing and shelter as a birth-right, work or no work. (*CL,* 322–23)

These early letters are particularly fascinating if read in light of *Rainbow,* which Lawrence started in March 1913, immediately after *Sons and Lovers* was published. The later novel ends with Ursula rejecting any connection with society, just as Lawrence himself was beginning to doubt the desirability or even the possibility of social action. The division in Lawrence's thinking between public and private commitments dominated the author's work to the end. This contradiction explains why in works such as *Rainbow* and *Plumed Serpent,* realism and mysticism battle to the last page. In the three *Lady Chatterley* versions, sexual and roman-

Introduction 13

tic passion conflicts with the gamekeeper's social consciousness. These social and sexual contradictions were never resolved, and they provide the thematic dynamism for Lawrence's works, even when he camouflaged questions of class and society with psychology, religion, or sex.

Despite the deep-rooted presence of class in Lawrence's works, virtually no full-length study exists that traces the presence and development of class in Lawrence. Much recognition should go to Scott Sanders for his unique analysis, which breaks down the author's world view into the "fundamental opposition between nature and culture."[1] Sanders's thesis is that within this dichotomy, many of the social and class conflicts that so fascinated Lawrence can be found. But Sanders's book stands alone in the vast canon of Lawrentian criticism, and even Sanders does not fully acknowledge the complexity within Lawrence's work. For example, Sanders's somewhat accusing argument that *Lady Chatterley's Lover* represents in the end a flight from history "into a mythical realm in which the passions of the body redeem the cruelties of the world" does not give Lawrence enough credit.[2] Not wholly satisfied by the way *Lady Chatterley* ended, Lawrence wrote three separate versions. If we trust the tale and not the artist, even the least political version—the final one—suggests that a retreat from history or society into a mythic realm of sex or blood consciousness was an inadequate response to a political problem. Lawrence's novels reveal more about class, society, and the individual than critics acknowledge.

In another, related area, critics are also neglectful. Lawrence's world view was continually modified by the great political developments of the day: by the First World War, the 1917 Bolshevik Revolution, and by the sporadic British labor strikes before and after the war. Lawrence wrote in July 1927, "I think societal instinct much deeper than sex instinct—and societal repression much more devastating" (*CL*, 989). This so-called instinct was subject to the ebb and flow of history as the subjects of his novels testify. Few critics acknowledge the influence of these sentiments on his work. One of these emerging trends was a deep mistrust and fear of the mob, which he held accountable for the war. The national chauvinism that he saw on both sides of the English Channel provoked Lawrence's generalized enmity:

The war makes me depressed [he wrote in a letter to Gordon Campbell in September 1914], the talk about the war makes me sick, and I have never come so near to hating mankind as I am now. They are fools, and vulgar fools, and cowards who will always make a noise because they are afraid of the silence. I don't even mind if they're killed. But I do mind those who, being sensitive, will receive such a blow from the ghastliness and mechanical, obsolete, hideous stupidity of war, that they will be crippled beings further burdening our sick society. Those that die, let them die. But those that live afterwards—the thought of them makes me sick. (*CL*, 290–291)

Nevertheless, he understood the futility of the individual acting in isolation, and he wanted a change in the social system. In 1915 he envisioned a new community that would allow the full development of the individual, but a community in which "the ultimate satisfaction and joy is in the completeness of us all" (*CL*, 311). He explained the impossibility of separating the good of one from the good of all; it was necessary to submerge personal interests and material interests to the common good. However, a community of interests did not include the British people as a whole, only a few "natural" aristocrats. The masses were still the enemy. Society had to change and man alone was a hopeless thing. To Lady Morell, in February 1915, he wrote:

> I do hope that we shall all of us be able to agree, that we have a common way, a common interest, not a private way and a private interest only.
> It is communism based, not on poverty, but on riches, not on humility but on pride, not on sacrifice but upon complete fulfillment in the flesh of all strong desire, not in Heaven but on earth. We will be Sons of God who walk here on earth, not bent on getting and having, because we know we inherit all things. We will be aristocrats, and as wise as the serpent in dealing with the mob. For the mob shall not crush us nor starve us nor cry us to death. We will deal cunningly with the mob, the greedy soul, we will gradually bring it to subjection. (*CL*, 311–12)

The same month he was deploring the rabble, Lawrence spoke of the need for a social revolution, for a revolutionary party.

In the early years of the war, before he and Frieda were accused of spying for Germany and before he had to report for military service, Lawrence had called repeatedly for two things: a revolutionary change in society and the need for men to give up their social aloofness. Lawrence later switched his passions to a denunciation of the war-mad mob, but, in 1915, Lawrence wrote that "a vision of a better life must include a revolution of society." Fur-

Introduction 15

thermore, he said, "The ultimate passion of every man is to be within himself the whole of mankind—which I call social passion—which is what brings to fruit your philosophical writings" (*CL*, 324). In March 1915, the month he finished *Rainbow*, Lawrence told Lady Ottoline Morrell that for change to come, men must act together or perish individually:

> No one man can create a new race. It needs all of us. So we must all unite for this purpose. It makes me quite glad to think how splendid it will be, when more and more of us fasten our hands on the chains, and pull, and pull, and break them apart. (*CL*, 325)

Between February and March 1915, Lawrence began to spin a rather complex web of conflicting attachments: to an elite, to the larger community, and to revolutionary change.

By the second half of 1915, Lawrence had dramatically reversed himself. Rather than endorse militant social change, Lawrence expressed fear about postwar class struggle: "Unless real leaders step forward, to lead in the light of a wide-embracing philosophy, there will be another French Revolution muddle" (*CL*, 351). Thereafter, Lawrence continued to express his fears of a worker take-over. He blamed the jingoism of the masses for the continuation of the war. In the sporadic miners' strikes he saw nothing but a one-sided interest in materialism. In his "Preface to *Touch and Go*," a play he completed in 1918, Lawrence described the struggle between workers and owners as one between "that old bulldog, the British capitalist," and "that unsatisfied mongrel, Plebs, the proletariat." "The one is all head and arrogance, the other all paws and grudge." The "bone" of property "is only the pretext." The worker is "the old Shylock" who wants his pound of flesh from the boss, and the latter simply wants to keep his property intact and for himself (*Ph 2*, 292).

The war corrupted Lawrence's best instincts; by 1915 he equated Western democracy with everything he loathed or feared: the war itself, jingoism, a mindless greed for money and property, rule by anarchistic masses, and a materialist outlook that precluded art and the growth of the individual. He identified the democratic cause with Russell, against whom Lawrence became increasingly embittered:

> You must drop all your democracy. You must not believe in "the people." One class is no better than another. It must be a case of

16   CLASS, POLITICS, AND THE INDIVIDUAL

> Wisdom, or Truth. Let the working classes *be* working classes. That is the truth. There must be an aristocracy of people who have wisdom, and there must be a Ruler: a Kaiser: no Presidents and democracies. I shall write out Herakleitos, on tablets of bronze. (*CL*, 352)

Democracy would inevitably lead, Lawrence feared, to a dictatorship of the working class. In another letter that same month, again to Russell:

> Can't you see the whole state is collapsing? Look at the Welsh strike. This war is going to develop into the last great war between labour and capital. It will be a ghastly chaos of destruction, if it is left to Labour to be constructive. The fight must immediately be given a higher aim than the triumph of Labour, or we shall have another French Revolution. The deadly Hydra now is the hydra of Equality. Liberty, Equality and Fraternity is the three-fanged serpent. You must have a government based upon good, better and best. (*CL*, 353–54)

By the end of the month Lawrence had uttered his most reactionary statement to date. The state, he wrote Russell, "must culminate in one real head . . . no foolish republics with foolish presidents, but an elected king, something like Julius Caesar. . . . There must be an elected aristocracy" (*CL*, 355–56). The war, Lawrence's sudden and dangerous decline in health, and the persecutions against him (in November 1915, a judge ordered all copies of *Rainbow* destroyed) had undone him.

These wartime letters reveal the issues that were tearing Lawrence apart and that figure so profoundly in his fiction. His correspondence pulses with equally intense but conflicting passions. Lawrence spoke almost simultaneously of his generalized hatred of all mankind and his desire to "send up the shoots of a new era: a great, utter revolution, and the dawn of a new historical epoch: either that, or the vast amorphous dust" (*CL*, 374). In these wartime letters he no longer differentiated between workers and masters. He suffered because he wished so desperately for radical social change but could attach himself neither to the middle class—whom he accused of wanting to continue "in this state of disintegration wherein each separate little ego is an independent little principality by itself" (*CL*, 360)—nor to any working-class movement. He was "too sick of world builders" (*CL*, 542), particularly of the democratic sort. But the day after making this statement, Lawrence wrote: "I feel nothing but a quite bloody, merciless, almost anarchistic revolution will be any good for this country; a

Introduction 17

fearful chaos of smashing up. . . . I know it *should* come, and must come; yet I would like to go away, not to see it" (*CL*, 542–43).

The key to these ambivalences was Lawrence's love-hate relationship with the British worker. *Sons and Lovers, Women in Love, Lost Girl,* and *Aaron's Rod,* all written between 1913 and 1917, reflect his divided feelings. No critic was more explicit about this split in his passions than Lawrence himself:

> Altogether the life here [Derbyshire] is so dark and violent; it all happens in the senses, powerful and rather destructive: no mind nor mental consciousness, unintellectual. These men are passionate enough, sensuous, dark-God, how all my boyhood comes back—so violent, so dark, the mind always dark and without understanding, the senses violently active. It makes me sad beyond words. These men, whom I love so much—and the life has such a power over me—they *understand* mentally so horribly: only industrialism, only wages and money and machinery. They can't *think* anything else. All their collective thinking in those terms only. [. . .]
>
> The strange, dark, sensual life, so violent, and hopeless at the bottom, combined with this horrible paucity and materialism of mental consciousness, makes me so sad, I could scream. They are still so living, so vulnerable, so darkly passionate. I love them like brothers—but, my God I hate them too. (*CL*, 404–5)

When the Lawrences took a cottage in Cornwall, all of the author's nightmares about being submerged in the darkness, passion, and mindlessness of workers came true. For a time, as he described in the chapter called "Nightmare" in *Kangaroo,* Lawrence and Frieda were spied upon by men who thought the couple was sending signals to offshore German submarines. Nevertheless, Lawrence continued to write that "the Cornish people still attract me. They have become detestable, I think, and yet they *aren't* detestable." They were a race, he thought, like workers in general, in which "is left some of the old sensuousness of the darkness, a sort of softness, a sort of flowing together in physical intimacy, something almost negroid, which is fascinating" (*CL*, 418–19). But "they are entirely mindless," Lawrence concluded, and "they ought all to die."

Other conflicts that dominated Lawrence's works during and after the war spring from the author's profound ambivalence toward working people and the part they might play in transforming society. The first such conflict—part hope and part nightmare—was that England was going to have and needed to have its own war, a revolutionary war. This theme was the backdrop of *Aaron's Rod,* published in 1922. Another was his fear that the passion of workers was based in part on their mindlessness, which strangled individuality. Lawrence described with morbid fascination what it was like to be among British recruits when he was called up for a preinduction physical examination:

> The ignominy is horrible, the humiliation. And even this terrible glamour of Homer and of all militarism, is a decadence, a degradation, a losing of individual form and distinction, a merging in the sticky male mass. It attracts me for a moment, but immediately, what a degradation and a prison, oh intolerable. I could not *bear* it—I should die in a week if they made me a soldier. Thirty men in their shirts, being weighed like sheep, one after the other—God! They have such impossible feet. (*CL,* 456)

Finally, perhaps as a justification for staying out of class conflict, Lawrence equated the British people with their rulers as the war dragged on past 1916, the year Lawrence was so certain it would end. For the protraction of the war he blamed worker and industrialist, soldier and officer equally. By 1917 the sun had gone out of the sky for Lawrence, and no positive social change seemed possible. The British government, he wrote, was "determined to prosecute the war indefinitely." The military authorities "are in the filthiest state of bloodthirstiness." As for the people, they go

> from bad to worse. It is impossible to believe in any existing body, they are all part of the same evil game, labour, capital, aristocrat, they are the trunk, limbs, and head of one body of destructive evil. How can one say, the head is to blame, but the trunk is blameless? They are all one thing. (*CL,* 511)

As always, Lawrence's work told a different tale. A major key toward the understanding of virtually everything Lawrence was then writing and wrote until his death can be found in his complex attitudes toward labor and capital, revolutionary change, and the isolation of the self from that change. Though class-related issues often seem to be subordinate to psychological or sexual matters— as in *Women in Love* and *Lady Chatterley's Lover*—even within private relationships Lawrence hears the echoes of social rumblings. The modern age made individual freedom the grand illusion of our time, and these works testify that Lawrence recognized this illusion, perhaps better than any of his contemporaries.

Introduction 19

The ghost that most haunted Lawrence was neither sexual nor psychological but social. Tormented by industrialism and the impossibility of choosing sides in class struggle, he was forever the Titan "nailed on the rock of the modern industrial capitalistic system," as this famous 1927 letter made clear:

> What ails me is the absolute frustration of my primeval societal instinct. The hero illusion starts with the individualistic illusion, and all resistances ensue. I think societal instinct much deeper than sex instinct—and societal repression much more devastating. There is no repression of the sexual individual comparable to the repression of the societal man in me, by the individual ego, my own and everybody else's. I am weary even of my own individuality, and simply nauseated by other people's (*CL*, 989–90).

The societal instinct battled Lawrence's heroic illusion—the desire to be his own man, free from society—in all of his major works. The critics who overlook this insist that Lawrence's main concerns were religious, sexual, or psychological. Political questions become for many readers of Lawrence, metaphysical ones. It is a curious fact, for example, one rarely considered by critics, that the original gamekeeper in *The First Lady Chatterley* was a communist organizer for his union, and that Mellors becomes an officer and a gentleman only by the third version of the novel. Even then, Lady Chatterley's lover talks as much about the horrors of industrial England as he does about the redemptive nature of intimacy and sex.

It is hardly possible to read Lawrence during any period of his life without recognizing how strongly he felt that a radical change in Western civilization had to occur before the individual could reach his potential in his private or social life. No sexual, psychological, or artistic growth seemed possible to him under modern industrialism with its fundamentally exploitative social, economic, and sexual relationships. That is why in Lawrence's novels, plays, and short stories an unbreakable link exists between the sufferings and conflicts his characters experience and the social setting in which they find themselves.

In *Studies in Classic American Literature*, in the chapter called "The Spirit of the Place," Lawrence cautioned the reader to be aware of the "subterfuge" of art. "An artist," he wrote, "is usually a damned liar, but his art, if it be art, will tell you the truth of his day. And that is all that matters." Every major hero that Lawrence created—Paul Morel, Ursula Brangwen, Rupert Birkin, Aaron Sis-

20 CLASS, POLITICS, AND THE INDIVIDUAL

son, Kate Leslie, and Oliver Mellors—solemnly affirmed their freedom from a political society they profoundly mistrusted, all the while they were set inextricably in a rich social setting. But no single character can be said to be a spokesman for Lawrence. "Men are free," Lawrence made clear in "The Spirit of the Place," "when they are escaping to some wild west." The truth of the day that Lawrence's works bear witness to was that the great social, political, and class-related issues of our time have to be squarely faced before we can begin to say we understand ourselves.

Notes

1. Scott Sanders, *D. H. Lawrence: The World of the Five Major Novels* (New York: Viking Press, 1973), p. 13.
2. Ibid., p. 205.

Class,
Politics,
and the Individual

1

Society and the Individual: *Sons and Lovers, The Rainbow,* and *Women in Love*

Social Class and the Individual in *Sons and Lovers*

Sons and Lovers, Lawrence's first major novel, has almost as complex a history as does his last major work, *Lady Chatterley's Lover,* which underwent three rewritings. His first novel was written twice, although its complexion probably did not undergo quite so radical a change as did the *Chatterley* works. *Sons and Lovers* was eventually finished in November 1912 and published the following year.

Lawrence revised *Sons and Lovers* for the same reasons he wrote three versions of *Lady Chatterley:* he was undecided as to the importance of class as a theme in his novels. In *Sons and Lovers,* as with the *Chatterley* novels, the issue of class centers in the novels' principal male characters: Paul and his father, Walter Morel, in *Sons and Lovers,* and the gamekeeper, called Parkin in *The First Lady Chatterley,* later Mellors in *Lady Chatterley's Lover.* The changes in the characterizations of Walter Morel and the gamekeeper have to do with Lawrence's fluctuating attitudes toward the significance of social class as a determinant of individual development and the extent to which he identified with workers. *Sons and Lovers* is the first full-length expression of Lawrence's developing and often contradictory statements about class and interpersonal relationships. Virtually every subsequent novel explored these divisions in Lawrence's thinking.

23

24 CLASS, POLITICS, AND THE INDIVIDUAL

In his essays, too, Lawrence never stopped rewriting *Sons and Lovers;* he was constantly revising, justifying, or explaining its themes of sons and lovers, sons as lovers, and husbands and wives. This last dichotomy particularly held his attention. In two auto-biographical sketches, Lawrence reflected on this theme, which so preoccupied him in *Sons and Lovers.* In "Autobiographical Fragment," written in 1927, and in "Autobiographical Sketch," written the following year, Lawrence clarified the husband-wife conflict: it was not, he claimed, exclusively psychological or sexual, but deeply social as well. Husbands and wives often had conflicting class aspirations, as Morel and Gertrude clearly do in *Sons and Lovers.*

In "Fragment," Lawrence is sympathetic to the men of his father's generation. Despite the brutality and drunkenness of colliers like Walter Morel, they were never, in Lawrence's words, "got under"; they behaved the way he sometimes wanted workers to behave: with a certain class militancy. "Fragment" describes women with bourgeois aspirations, including a social decency that Lawrence scorns, who dominate their husbands. The description in "Fragment" is strikingly close to the ambivalent way Lawrence portrays both Gertrude and Walter Morel in *Sons and Lovers.* In "Fragment," the author compares the colliers of Newthorpe to the miners of his father's generation:

> The colliers of today are the men of my generation, lads I went to school with. I find it hard to believe. They were rough, wild lads. They are not rough, wild men. The board-school, the Sunday-school, the Band of Hope, and above all, their mothers got them under. Got them under, made them tame. Made them sober, conscientious, and decent. Made them good husbands. [. . .]
> The decent colliers of my generation are got under entirely. They are so patient, so forebearing, so willing to listen to reason, so ready to put themselves aside. [. . .] There they are, poor as their fathers before them, but poor with a hopeless outlook and a new and expensive world around them. (*Ph 1,* 817–18)

In "Autobiographical Sketch," Lawrence details virtually all the class-related themes that he began to probe in *Sons and Lovers.* To his father he ascribes a certain amount of social rudeness, of which Lawrence came grudgingly to admire. His mother was "superior," but in a way the author came to regard with suspicion and even scorn:

Society and the Individual   25

> I was born among the working classes and brought up among them. My father was a collier, and only a collier, in so far as he got drunk rather frequently, never went near a chapel, and was usually rather rude to his little immediate bosses at the pit.
>
> He practically never had a good stall all the time he was a butty, because he was always saying tiresome and foolish things about the men just above him in control at the mine. He offended them all, almost on purpose, so how could he expect them to favor him? Yet he grumbled when they didn't.
>
> My mother was, I suppose, superior. She came from town, and belonged really to the lower bourgeoisie. She spoke the King's English, without an accent, and never in her life could even imitate a sentence of the dialect which my father spoke, and which we children spoke out of doors. (*Ph* 2, 592)

"She was very much respected," Lawrence concludes, "just as my father was not respected. Her nature was quick and sensitive, and perhaps really superior" (*Ph* 2, 593).

A few months after he finished "Autobiographical Sketch," Lawrence wrote a poetry collection called *Pansies*, where he wrote at length about class expectations and class-related values. In "Prestige," Lawrence spoke about the middle-class quality of prestige, which he called superiority. The narrator worries that he is unable to get in touch with this "mysterious sort of prestige." The second half of the poem reads as follows:

> For years and years it bothered me
> that I couldn't feel one of them,
> till at last I saw the reason,
> they were just a bloody sham.
>
> As far as any superiority
> or halo or prestige went
> they were just a bloody collective fraud,
> that was what their *"Ahem!"* meant.
>
> Their superiority was meanness,
> they were cunning about the goods
> and sly with a lot of after-thought,
> and they put it over us, the duds!
>
> And I'd let myself be swindled
> half believing 'em till one day
> I suddenly said: I've finished!
> My God, let me get away!

(stanzas 6–9)

26 CLASS, POLITICS, AND THE INDIVIDUAL

Sons and Lovers does not go this far in rejecting the values of Lawrence's mother and her bourgeois superiority. But part of Paul's ability to resist his mother involves the author's recognition of his father's vitality and passion, qualities Lawrence identified closely with the working class.

Toward the conclusion of "Autobiographical Sketch," Lawrence outlines most of the class ambivalencies he struggled with in *Sons and Lovers* and, indeed, during his lifetime:

> As a man from the working class, I feel that the middle class cut off some of my vital vibration when I am with them. I admit them charming and educated and good people often enough. *But they just stop some part of me from working.* [italics in original] Some part has to be left out.
>
> Then why don't I live with my working people? Because their vibration is limited in another direction. They are narrow, but still fairly deep and passionate, whereas the middle class is broad and shallow and passionless. Quite passionless. At the best, they substitute affection, which is the great middle-class positive emotion.
>
> But the working class is narrow in outlook, in prejudice, and narrow in intelligence. This again makes a prison. One can belong absolutely to no class. (*Ph 1,* 595)

This passage is indicative of one of Lawrence's lifetime concerns: finding an acceptable relationship to his class. Because he had a love-hate feeling toward workers, and toward his father in particular, Lawrence continually rewrote the character of Morel. The extreme ambivalence with which Lawrence describes workers in "Autobiographical Sketch" is consistent with his portrayal of workers throughout his major works. It is therefore surprising that so many critics write about *Sons and Lovers* with only a perfunctory acknowledgment of the importance of social class as a significant motif.

Generally critics do not credit Lawrence with the understanding that man's sexual and psychological make-up is rooted in a social setting. From the very first pages of *Sons and Lovers,* for example, the reader is clearly shown how Morel's intense sexuality and attractiveness are identified with his being a worker and not held back like the middle class, a point upon which Lawrence was quite unambiguous. If *Sons and Lovers* proves anything, it is that one's "vital self" is always in flux. It is a strength, not a weakness, in this novel that Lawrence constantly probes the questions of class and

Society and the Individual 27

sex, society and industrial relations on the one hand, and the conflicts between husband and wife, son and mother, son and lover on the other. Lawrence continually explored the connections between personal behavior and a social milieu. The fact that *Rainbow*, his next novel, or *Women in Love*, completed in November 1916, is almost antithetical to *Sons and Lovers* in its view of the individual's role in society, testifies to Lawrence's unresolved feelings about the importance of participating in society, the value of any sort of politics, and the possibility of sustaining an intimate relationship within an oppressive social context.

The subject matter of *Sons and Lovers* was so close to Lawrence that in many ways he never stopped rewriting it. A number of these recastings have already been mentioned; these later writings are valuable because they speak to the themes that Lawrence himself regarded as paramount. Perhaps the most fundamental of these themes in *Sons and Lovers* is the complexity and difficulty of sustaining relationships within an industrial environment that makes the fulfillment of human potentiality virtually impossible. Although a number of critics have sensed the connections between the psychological, sexual, and social forces in this book, few treat the subject at any length; few as well are inclined to credit Lawrence with knowing what exactly he was doing.

"Nottingham and the Mining Countryside," written in the summer of 1929, explicitly relates the sexual tensions found in *Sons and Lovers* to various material contradictions. In this essay, Lawrence proves the superficiality of separating out the book's multiple personal conflicts from the turn-of-the-century mining world in which the Morel family is a virtual prisoner. Both in the essay and in the novel, Nottinghamshire is "a queer jumble of old England and the new. [. . .] Life was a curious cross between industrialism and the old agricultural England of Shakespeare and Milton and Fielding and George Eliot" (*Ph 1*, 135). *Sons and Lovers*, like *Rainbow*, which follows it, describes this shattering economic and social transformation: "Some sixty years ago, a sudden change took place. The gin-pits were elbowed aside by the large mines of the financiers. The coal and iron field of Nottinghamshire and Derbyshire was discovered" (*SL*, 1). When Paul and Miriam discover the delights of natural beauty, they are not admiring an abstraction. Rather they are attemping to relive a quieter time that has been lost forever. Throughout *Sons and Lovers*, Lawrence uses nature to contrast the dreariness and ugliness of this new industrial life:

28   CLASS, POLITICS, AND THE INDIVIDUAL

Already [Paul] was a prisoner of industrialism. Large sunflowers stared over the old red wall of the garden opposite, looking in their jolly way down on the women who were hurrying with something for dinner. The valley was full of corn, brightening in the sun. Two collieries, among the fields, waved their small white plumes of steam. Far off on the hills were the woods of Annesley, dark and fascinating. Already his heart went down. He was being taken into bondage. His freedom in the beloved home valley was going now. (*SL*, 89)

Everyone is trapped, and no one seems certain upon what to build a future. The strain upon the family and upon intimate relationships is beginning to be felt. *Sons and Lovers* starts with this dilemma: unable to go backwards in time, the younger generation in particular has very little by which to be guided.

Both in the novel and in the essay, Lawrence describes a major effect of this social dislocation as the conflict between the instinctual, communal life of the men, and the more material aspirations of the women. The men worked and the wives aspired to escape the drudgery of working-class life through culture, religion, and wealth, items the colliers bitterly opposed. Lawrence regarded the challenge to the colliers' old way of life as a threat to life itself:

The people lived almost entirely by instinct, men of my father's age could not really read. And the pit did not mechanize men. On the contrary. Under the butty system, the miners worked underground as a sort of intimate community, they knew each other practically naked, and with curious intimacy, and the darkness and the underground remoteness of the pit "stall," and the continual presence of danger, made the physical, instinctive, and intuitional contact between men very highly developed, a contact almost as touch, very real and very powerful. This physical awareness and intimate *togetherness* was at its strongest down pit. When the men came up into the light, they blinked. They had, in a measure, to change their flow. Nevertheless, they brought with them above ground, the curious dark intimacy of the mine, the naked sort of contact, and if I think of my childhood, it is always as if there was a lustrous sort of inner darkness, like the gloss of coal, in which we moved and had our real being. My father loved the pit. He was hurt badly, more than once, but he would never stay away. He loved the intense male comradeship of the dark days. They did not know what they had lost till they lost it. (*Ph 1*, 135–36)

Industrialism affected the wives in a wholly opposite way. Detached from the work itself, according to Lawrence, they acquired class aspiration. They began to boss their collier husbands in a way

Society and the Individual 29

that resembled the social system of workers and owners. The wage system added ugliness, materialism, and sexual torment, where before, Lawrence observed, a certain harmony and passion had existed between man and nature, men and women:

> The great fallacy is, to pity the man. He didn't dream of pitying himself, till the agitators and sentimentalists taught him to. He was happy; or more than happy, he was fulfilled. Or he was fulfilled on the receptive side, not on the expressive. The collier went to the pub and drank in order to continue his intimacy with his mates. [. . .]
> The collier fled out of the house as soon as he could, away from the nagging materialism of the woman. With the women it was always: This is broke, now you've got to mend it or else: we want this, that and the other, and where is the money to come from? The collier didn't know and didn't care very deeply—his life was otherwise. So he escaped. (*Ph 1*, 136)

As industrialism began to pull their lives apart, the men clung to what they knew best and what, for them, had some sort of passion. Having no class aspirations, Morel is shut out of his family by their attempts at culture, education, and social manners. For him, and for the men of his generation generally, Morel can define himself only through work—the one thing the new industrial order has not taken from him:

> The only times when he entered again into the life of his own people was when he worked, and was happy at work. Sometimes, in the evening, he cobbled the boots, or mended the kettle or his pit-bottle. Then he always wanted several attendants, and the children enjoyed it. They united with him in the work, in the actual doing of something, when he was his real self again. (*SL*, 63)

The women could share in none of this, and the result is that every male-female relationship in *Sons and Lovers* is marked by this disjointedness. Gertrude deals with Paul and her husband in a way that parallels Miriam's relationship with Paul. They try to subsume what they see as masculine defiance or sensuality into more polite, socially acceptable behavior. The differences in style, temperament, and passion is made evident early in the novel:

> There began a battle between the husband and wife—a fearful, bloody battle that ended only with the death of one. She fought to make him undertake his own responsibilities, to make him fulfil his obligations. But he was too different from her. His nature was purely

sensuous, and she strove to make him moral, religious. She tried to force him to face things. He could not endure it—it drove him out of his mind. (*SL*, 14)

As a young boy, Paul begins to pick up on his mother's arrogance toward the colliers. In one scene, Paul has to stand in line with the rest of the miners to pick up his father's paycheck. He comes back deeply injured. "They're hateful, and common, and hateful, they are, and I'm not going anymore," Paul tells his mother. "Mr. Braithwaite drops his 'h's', an' Mr. Winterbottom says 'You was' " (*SL*, 72).

When Morel, asserting what he perceives to be his masculine paternal duty, clips his infant son's hair, all the nascent antagonism between his parents surface. Neither is the villain, but their differences are irreconcilable:

This act of masculine clumsiness was the spear through the side of her love for Morel. Before, while she had striven against him bitterly, she had fretted after him, as if he had gone astray from her. Now she ceased to fret for his love: he was an outsider to her. This made life much more bearable.[. . .]

The pity was, she was too much his opposite. She could not be content with the little he might be; she would have him the much that he ought to be. So, in seeking to make him nobler than he could be, she destroyed him. (*SL*, 16)

Although the narrator may often side with Gertrude's rejection of Morel's apparent coarseness, Lawrence presents an opposing case. Morel's brutality is not only a reaction to his having worked in the pits since he was ten, it is also the only way he knows how to save his manhood. Miriam and Clara are attracted to Paul for the same reason Gertrude was initially attracted to Walter Morel. The men have a vitality and rebelliousness that is denied to most of the women. Lawrence's description of the young Gertrude is not unlike his description of Miriam:

[Gertrude] was puritan, like her father, high-minded, and really stern. Therefore the dusky, golden softness of this man's sensuous flame of life, that flowed off his flesh like the flame from a candle, not baffled and gripped into incandescence by thought and spirit as her life was, seemed to her something wonderful, beyond her. (*SL*, 10)

Walter seemed "noble" to her. "He risked his life daily and with gaiety." The split between husband and wife, mother and son, and

Society and the Individual 31

son and lover begins when the women attempt to fashion the men in their image, into a social model that Lawrence perceived to be passionless, abstract, willful, and consuming, traits he later, in *Women in Love,* for example, identified directly with the middle class.

Morel is alternately brutal and tender toward his family: he is mortified when he drunkenly assails his wife and sickened with misery when his son William dies. Yet for all the ambivalence with which Lawrence portrays the worker Morel, his portrayal of William's "ascent" into the middle class of Bestwood and then London has nothing redemptive about it. William's gradual slide into alienation, depression, and death begins when he takes up "with the bourgeoisie of Bestwood" and consorts with people who are utterly foreign (because socially superior) to him. William aggressively pursues the dream Gertrude later hands to Paul, "to climb into the middle classes, a thing not very difficult she knew. And she wanted him in the end to marry a lady" (*SL*, 256). William, however, comes to feel that his desertion of the Bottoms was, like Lawrence's poem about his encounter with the middle class, a betrayal. The first two stanzas of "Climbing Up" describe, in effect, what happened to William:

> When you climb up to the middle classes
> you leave a lot behind you,
> you leave a lot, you've lost a lot
> and you've nobody to remind you
> of all the things they squeezed out of you
> when they took you and refined you.
>
> When they took you and refined you
> they squeezed out most of your guts;
> they took away your good old stones
> and gave you a couple of nuts;
> and they taught you to speak King's English
> and butter your slippery buts.

The fifth and sixth stanzas reflect Lawrence's lifelong contempt for a class he felt was robbing the Morels of his generation of their manhood, their vitality:

> You think they're the same as you are
> and then you find they're not,
> and they never were nor would be,
> not one of the whole job lot.

32 CLASS, POLITICS, AND THE INDIVIDUAL

And you have to act up like they do
or they think you're off your dot.

There isn't a man among 'em,
not one; they all seemed to me
like monkeys or angels or something, in a limited
liability company;
like a limited liability company
they are, all limited liability.

Lawrence is not nearly as militant in his novel as he is in many of his poems in *Pansies* where he rails against the bourgeoisie. But *Sons and Lovers* does begin to probe the differences and aspirations that exist between Lawrence's male and female characters, differences in values that he believed originated in class.

Morel works in the mines, and Paul and Baxter Dawes work in a factory that makes surgical appliances. Of the three major female characters—Gertrude, Miriam, and Clara—only Clara works in industry. As a result, she is often treated more sympathetically. "There's a sort of fierceness somewhere in her," Paul observes when he first meets her, a fierceness, like Morel's, that immediately attracts him. "She's got a grudge against men," Miriam tells Paul, and, as the narrator explains, "That was probably one of his own reasons for liking Mrs. Dawes, but this did not occur to him" (*SL*, 187). Just as Morel "can't understand rules and regulations," as Gertrude complains to Paul, Clara revolts against those who have limited her freedom. She was separated from her husband "and had taken up Women's Rights." In *Sons and Lovers*, Lawrence puts a high premium on workers' defiance of authority, which is one reason Clara is such an appealing figure to Paul.

Miriam, on the other hand, is not as vital a figure. She is less intimate, less assertive, and more abstract—qualities Lawrence identified with the upper classes. Mrs. Leivers resembles Gertrude insofar as they both attempt to foster the same spiritual values upon their children, the former with far greater success. Miriam's mother has many of Gertrude's class expectations, which means, in effect, that both women demean their men.

[The Leivers women] were both brown-eyed, and inclined to be mystical, such women as treasure religion inside them, breathe it in their nostrils, and see the whole of life in a mist thereof. So to Miriam, Christ and God made one great figure, which she loved tremblingly and passionately when a tremendous sunset burned out the western sky [. . .]; she went to church reverently, with bowed head, and

Society and the Individual   33

quivered in anguish from the vulgarity of the other choir-girls and from the common-sounding voice of the curate; she fought with her brothers, whom she considered brutal louts; and she held not her father in too high esteem because he did not carry any mystical ideals cherished in his heart, but only wanted to have as easy a time as he could, and his meals when he was ready for them. (*SL*, 142–43)

Lawrence says of Miriam, "She must have something to reinforce her pride, because she felt different from other people. Paul she eyed rather wistfully. On the whole, she scorned the male sex" (*SL*, 143). Mrs. Leivers undercuts her sons in a way that parallels Gertrude's scorn of most of the colliers. "They are such brutes," Miriam says of her brothers. "They're so hateful! and—low." "Yes, dear," her mother replies (*SL*, 147). All the latent and apparent class snobbery of Gertrude is refined to a high degree in Miriam, a quality that alienates her from her brothers and that, ultimately, makes inevitable her split from Paul. She is too much— for the men around her, that is—a product of her mother's anti-working-class upbringing:

> Miriam was exceedingly sensitive, as her mother had always been. The slightest grossness made her recoil almost in anguish. Her brothers were brutal, but never coarse in speech. The men did all the discussing of farm matters outside. But, perhaps, because of the continual business of birth and of begetting which goes on upon every farm, Miriam was the more hypersensitive to the matter, and her blood was chastened almost to disgust of the faintest suggestion of such intercourse. Paul took his pitch from her, and their intimacy went on in an utterly blanched and chaste fashion. (*SL*, 162)

The sexual conflicts, first between father and mother, and later between son and lover, are the occasions for describing class differences. Paul's sexuality, in conflict with Miriam's spirituality, reflects the struggle between working-class physicality and sociability, and bourgeois individualism and social elitism. The contrasts between Walter Morel and Gertrude foreshadow Paul and Miriam's relationship, and both relationships are grounded in class differences. Paul's relationship with Miriam follows the route his mother's marriage took. Morel's "purely sensuous" nature was challenged by a women who "strove to make him moral, religious." Similarly, Paul "felt that [Miriam] wanted the soul out of his body, and not him. All his strength and energy she drew into herself through some channel which united them. She did not want

34 CLASS, POLITICS, AND THE INDIVIDUAL

to meet him, so that there were two of them, man and woman together" (*SL*, 194). Paul's perpetual bitterness toward Miriam is that theirs is a relationship into which "no body enters." For the same reason, Miriam will have nothing to do with her brothers, because they have been brutalized by their work.

Lawrence expressed his own ambivalence about his class roots through Paul's conflicted attitude toward Miriam and toward Walter Morel, his father. Paul is both drawn to Miriam's etherealness and repelled by it. He is disgusted, as is his mother, by his father's coarseness and brutality. At the same time, Paul needs to satisfy his own sexual longings. One scene in particular describes this tug of war between Paul's sexuality and Miriam's spirituality. He is watching her as she sings:

> She sang like a nun singing to heaven. It reminded him so much of the mouth and eyes of one who sings beside a Botticelli Madonna, so spiritual. Again, hot as steel, came up the pain in him. Why must he ask her for the other thing? If only he could have been always gentle, tender with her, breathing with her the atmosphere of rêverie and religious dreams, he would give his right hand. It was not fair to hurt her. There seemed an eternal maidenhood about her. (*SL*, 279)

When Paul finally rejects Miriam, he returns to the physical, to what he calls "the real and vital part" of a man. He spurns an affection of "two souls," a love in which he is "a mystic monk" to Miriam's "mystic nun." In a social context, Paul's return to the somatic is also a return to physical labor, as opposed to Miriam's French and horticultural lessons. "I suppose work *can* be nearly everything to a man," Paul tells Miriam during their final encounter. "But a man can give *all* himself to work?" Miriam asks. "Yes, practically," Paul answers (*SL*, 416).

The age of industrialism has stripped men of nearly everything but their pride in their work. In addition to the contrast between how the major male and female characters in this book labor—the differences between, for example, men in industry and women at home or on the farm—Lawrence describes class differences in another, related way. A mind-body dichotomy becomes an appropriate metaphor to show class contradictions between the major characters. Paul and Miriam attach a great value to education and culture as means whereby they may escape the horrors of industrial drudgery. At the same time, Lawrence contrasts some of the freedom culture may offer with the dangers of industrial labor. In

Society and the Individual 35

Sons and Lovers, most of the male characters are either injured or killed outright by the effects of their work: Morel is repeatedly injured in the mines; William dies trying to climb the social ladder; and both Paul and Baxter are weakened and nearly die from fatigue. Workers can survive only so long as they can labor, and Lawrence is acutely aware of what industrialism does to their bodies. Part of the book is a chronicle of how men physically suffer, how their bodies are slowly ruined by work or illness. This is particularly true of Morel: "As he grew older, Morel fell into a slow ruin. His body, which had been beautiful in movement and in being, shrank, did not seem to ripen with the years, but to get mean and rather despicable. There came over him a look of meanness and paltriness" (*SL,* 113).

Sons and Lovers begins with this mind-body, middle-class–working-class dichotomy. Walter Morel is identified physically, establishing the metaphor of body as associated with workers:

> He had wavy black hair that shone again, and a vigorous black beard that had never been shaved. His cheeks were ruddy, and his red, moist mouth was noticable because he laughed so often and so heartily. He had that rare thing, a rich, ringing laugh. Gertrude Coppard had watched him, fascinated. He was so full of colour and animation, his voice ran so easily into comic grotesque, he was so ready and so pleasant with everybody. Her own father had a rich fund of humour, but it was satiric. This man was different: soft, non-intellectual, warm, a kind of gambolling. (*SL,* 9)

Similarly, Clara and Paul are attracted to one another's physicalness. Clara "was conscious of [Paul's] quick, vigorous body as it came and went, seeming blown quickly by a wind at its work" (*SL,* 322). Baxter Dawes—the third male character—has a worker's vibrancy, but, like Morel, he physically declines at an early age.

Paul is at the center of all these antagonisms: between the pull of his father's class and his mother's expectations; between physical labor, which he comes to both love and hate, and his work as an artist, work that offers him a respite from his factory job; from a cultured sensibility represented by Miriam, to the warmth and passion of the common people. Much of *Sons and Lovers* is a working out of Lawrence's conflicted sense that class does and does not make the man, that he should—though like Paul he could not—commit himself to his father's class. The mother-son and son-lover conflicts revolve around these tensions, as Paul and the

36 CLASS, POLITICS, AND THE INDIVIDUAL

narrator divide their loyalties between the cultural and intellectual refinements that Gertrude and Miriam stand for, and the vitality inherent in characters like Morel and Clara.

As Paul gains a perspective on his class, the gulf between himself and his mother widens. He begins to rebel when he realizes that Gertrude's prescription for social success will only kill the passion within him. Thus Lawrence sets into motion a theme that he thereafter incorporates into every one of his novels: the tragedy of life is not in hard work, personal suffering, or the need for struggle; it is in the failure to have lived to one's fullest potential. At one point Gertrude makes it clear to Paul that she wishes him to move up in society; that is where true happiness lies, she tells him. "I don't want to belong to the well-to-do middle class. I like my common people best. I belong to the common people," he tells her. "All your cleverness, your breaking away from old things, and taking life in your own hands, doesn't seem to bring you much happiness," Gertrude replies (*SL*, 257). Paul articulates what his father cannot express, although Morel's life is rich in the sort of vibrancy Paul comes to admire:

> "What is happiness! It's nothing to me! How *am* I to be happy?" [Paul asks his mother.]
> "That's for you to judge, my lad. But if you could meet some *good* woman who would *make* you happy—and you began to think of settling your life—when you have the means—so that you could work without all this fretting—it would be much better for you. . . ."
> "You mean easy, mother," he cried. "That's a woman's whole doctrine for life—ease of soul and physical comfort. And I do despise it."
> "Oh, do you!" replied his mother. "And do you call yours a divine discontent?"
> "Yes, I don't care about its divinity. But damn your happiness! So long as life's full, it doesn't matter whether it's happy or not. I'm afraid your happiness would bore me." (*SL*, 257)

In *Sons and Lovers*, by and large the only characters who suggest this sort of combativeness and energy are Morel, Clara and her mother, Baxter, and, upon occasion, Paul. They battle society and they pay a heavy price for it. The occasional gratuitous brutality of men like Morel and Dawes, which Gertrude's snobbery or Paul's elitism inevitably draws out, is never romanticized. Such bullying represents an aspect of working-class life that Lawrence detested, one that he portrayed repeatedly, especially in his wartime and immediate postwar novels. Nonetheless, in this novel he reserves

Society and the Individual   37

for workers a unique dignity, against which is contrasted, somewhat less sympathetically, Miriam's and Gertrude's moral and social aloofness.

Clara and her mother, Mrs. Radford, epitomize Lawrence's conflictive sympathies with workers. Their story parallels, to a degree, Paul's attempt to escape the confinements of industrialism. Whereas Paul finds a respite in nature, in his art work, in literature, Clara becomes a social activist. Through her, Paul connects with the socialist, suffragette, Unitarian people in Nottingham. Lawrence had not yet begun to formulate a strong opinion about political involvement, as Clara's on-again, off-again social militancy makes clear. But Clara and her mother are unmistakably working-class people, and it is this quality that Lawrence finds so appealing. Lawrence's description of Mrs. Radford recalls that of Morel: "There was something determined about her that he liked. Her face was falling loose, but her eyes were calm, and there was something strong in her that made it seem she was not old; merely her wrinkles and loose cheeks were an anachronism. She had the strength and sang-froid of a woman in the prime of life" (*SL*, 261). The scene where Paul meets Clara's mother for the first time is significant because it is the antithesis of his visits to the Willey Farm. Miriam and Mrs. Leivers are opposite in sensibilities from Clara and her mother. The Leivers are "exceedingly sensitive." The differences between the Radford and Leivers family are based on class: "She's a nice girl," Mrs. Radford tells Paul. "She's very nice, but she's a bit too much above this world to suit my fancy. . . . She'll never be satisfied till she's got wings and can fly over everybody's head, she won't" (*SL*, 261).

Of the three women in Paul's life—his mother, Miriam, and Clara—only Clara seems conscious of her place in society as a woman and as a worker. In many ways and in part for this reason, Clara is a complex character. At different times during the novel the author pities her, identifies with her, and patronizes her. Clara speaks about the inequities of piecework, the exploitation of labor, "the cruelty," as she puts it, "of men in their brute force," and the need for a feminist movement. She is separated from her husband and, rather openly, carries on a love affair with Paul. Perhaps most of all, Clara serves to remind the reader how a character's hopes and potential for a full life have been jettisoned by industrial labor:

She seemed denied and deprived of so much. And her arm moved mechanically, that should never have been subdued to a mechanism, and her head was bowed to the lace, that never should have been bowed. She seemed to be stranded there among the refuse that life has thrown away, doing her jennying. It was a bitter thing to her to be put aside by life, as if it had no use for her. No wonder she protested. (*SL*, 262).

Yet by the novel's end she returns, rather submissively, to her husband; furthermore, in contradiction to the autonomous life she led as a single person, she is handed back to Baxter by Paul. Women cannot maintain their freedom of movement as men can. In turn-of-the-century industrial England this was certainly true.

But Lawrence is signaling something other than the dependence of working women on men. Paul is being pulled in opposite directions by these women and what they come to represent to him. His mother promoted a type of individualism that she believes will provide an alternative to the brutalizing effects of industrial labor—a system to which she feels Morel has fallen victim. Miriam cultivates religious and aesthetic sensibilities that will insulate her from the coarseness of the world around her; nature, too, becomes such a refuge. Clara is a more complex character because, although she too wants to escape the drudgery of factory work, she knows her limitations. In contrast to the elitism that Paul picks up from his mother and from Miriam is the camaraderie he develops with Miriam's brothers and the easy friendships Morel has with his fellow workers. A split between communal and private concerns is a major theme in *Sons and Lovers,* and it too has a basis in class identification.

The divisions between rural and city life, between physical and mental labor, and between society and the individual were fundamental to all of Lawrence's works. The common denominator of these elements is class. None of Lawrence's characters develop fully apart from a class background; none leads an essentially declassed life. Paul is caught for a long time between his social roots and his wish to achieve individuation; his frustration at not being able to resolve this contradiction nearly causes him to go insane. By the time his mother dies, and the last hold his family has on him is severed, he realizes that "his life is unbalanced, as if it were going to smash into pieces" (*SL*, 368.). Rejecting the abstraction and spirituality that Miriam offers him, unable to see anything redemptive in the life for which his father was a model, Paul tells Dawes that "it's as if I was in a tangled sort of hole, rather dark and dreary, and no road anywhere" (*SL*, 403).

Society and the Individual 39

After his mother's death, Paul sees that he "*was* nothing himself" (*SL*, 412). "Beyond the town, the country, little smouldering spots for more towns . . . he had no place in it! Whatever spot he stood on, there he stood alone" (*SL*, 419). What later Lawrentian heroes try to turn into victory, notably Ursula in *Rainbow*, is a defeat for Paul. For characters like Ursula, Aaron, and Mellors, the achievment of selfhood despite society's restraints may be regarded as a test of their strength and defiance. For Paul, however, the gardens and the romance of the Willey Farm temporarily destroy his hold on life, leaving him "feeling unsubstantial, shadowy, as if he did not count for much in this concrete world" (*SL*, 408).

Sons and Lovers is perhaps Lawrence's most painful expression of the individual caught between the values of two social classes. Whether Paul is conscious of this fact is not the point. He is caught in a tug of war between his father's and his mother's class outlook. The impact of class is felt everywhere, from the frustrations and despairs of Gertrude and Clara who feel trapped by their poverty, to the men who are injured by their work or, in William's case, who are killed when they aspire to a class they have no heart for. Paul can find no refuge either in Miriam's sheltered world of culture and romance, or in the insensitivity of Morel's. Unable to reach his full intellectual capacity in his father's sensual, though restricted world, he is suffocated in Miriam's abstracted one. While Walter Morel's brutality is not compensated for by his passionate nature, Miriam's angelic goodness avails nothing, for she "took all and gave nothing. . . . she gave no living warmth" (*SL*, 293).

Subsequent heroes in Lawrence's works more or less accept social isolation as the price they must pay to remain individuals. While his mother is alive, Paul is tormented by what he sees as his imprisonment among ordinary working people: "The real agony was that he had nowhere to go, nothing to do, nothing to say, and *was* nothing himself. . . . There was something between him and them. He could not get into touch. He did not want them. . . . There was nowhere to go" (*SL*, 412).

At the conclusion of *Sons and Lovers*, Paul takes a decisive action—one that no other protagonist is able to do in Lawrence's subsequent novels, *Rainbow, Women in Love, Aaron's Rod,* and *Kangaroo:* the hero returns to communal life, to social responsibility. Self-isolation is a terror compared to the struggles of community and the material world. Apart from society, Paul is "at the core a nothingness, and yet nothing"; he may yet develop *within*

40   CLASS, POLITICS, AND THE INDIVIDUAL

society. In contrast to other Lawrence novels, where at the end the hero moves away from fellowship and social responsibility, Paul returns home: "he would not give in. Turning sharply, he walked towards the city's gold phosphorescence. His fists were shut, his mouth set fast. He would not take that direction, to the darkness, to follow her. He walks towards the faintly humming, glowing town, quickly" (*SL*, 420). The darkness represents his mother and death. To return to life, Paul returns to the city and to his people. For Lawrence, as *Rainbow* shows, the way to a new life is not always in such a direction.

Sons and Lovers does not resolve the contradiction it poses. The strength of the book lies in its ability—its negative capability—not to reach for easy answers to the questions of class and the individual. This work, as well as *Rainbow* and *Women in Love*, which follow, are generally the most well received of Lawrence's fiction. The three are characterized by a profound sensitivity to social class and its effect on the individual. These novels locate many of the problems faced by the protagonist attempting to develop his or her full potentiality in a social and economic system not geared to promote that development. *Sons and Lovers*, *Rainbow*, and *Women in Love* carefully trace family histories to show how social and personal change are interrelated. *Sons and Lovers* is artistically one of Lawrence's greatest achievements. This book and the two that follow indicate that his best fiction coincides with the times he was most responsive to class and to the public and private tensions it produced.

Social Development and the Individual in *The Rainbow*

The Rainbow had as many revisions as did the *Lady Chatterley* novels. It was begun in March 1913 as *The Sisters* and revised as *The Wedding Ring* in 1914. Revised as *The Rainbow*, the work was finished in March 1915 and published that same year. No certain documentation exists explaining the nature of these extensive rewrites. The three versions are not, like the *Lady Chatterley* versions, available, but it is clear from Lawrence's correspondence that he was as usual being pulled in opposite directions, directions that may account for his dissatisfaction with the novel's final shape.

In his much-quoted letter to Edward Garnett, Lawrence wrote that he was interested in what his female character (presumably

Society and the Individual 41

Ursula) "*is*—inhumanly, physiologically, materially . . . what she *is* as a phenomenon." Then at some length he explained how *Rainbow* was different from the nineteenth-century Russian novel:

> You mustn't look in my novel for the old stable *ego* of the character. There is another *ego*, according to whose action the individual is unrecognisable, and passes through, as it were, allotropic states which it needs a deeper sense than any we've been used to exercise, to discover are states of the same single radically unchanged element. (Like as diamond and coal are the same pure single element of carbon. The ordinary novel would trace the history of the diamond—but I say "Diamond, what! This is carbon." And my diamond might be coal or soot, and my theme is carbon.) You must not say my novel is shaky—it is not perfect, because I am not an expert in what I want to do. [. . .] Again I say, don't look for the development of the novel to follow the lines of certain characters: the characters fall into the form of some other rhythmic form, as when one draws a fiddle-bow across a fine tray delicately sanded, the sand takes lines unknown. (*CL*, 282)

Neither in this letter nor in any other is Lawrence clear as to what this "radically unchanged element" might be. In 1914, he wrote Gordon Campbell that

> life tends to take two streams, male and female, and only some female influence [. . .] can fertilise the soul of man to vision or being. Then the vision we're after, I don't know what it is—but it is something that contains awe and dread and submission, not pride or sensuous egotism and assertion. (*CL*, 291)

"We want to realise the tremendous *non-human* quality of life," he added. "It is wonderful." Nevertheless, both the novel and his correspondence project the very human and very social ideas that were battling in Lawrence's consciousness, a conflict that hardly resembled "the eternal stillness . . . deeper than change, and struggling" which the author felt was characteristic of Greek sculpture and a bit like his new novel.

One dichotomy that interested Lawrence was the split between man's mental consciousness and his "blood" consciousness.

> My great religion [he wrote to Ernest Collings in 1913] is a belief in the blood, the flesh, as being wiser than the intellect. We can go wrong in our minds. But what our blood feels and believes and says, is always true. The intellect is only a bit and a bridle. What do I care about knowledge. All I want is to answer to my blood, direct, without

42   CLASS, POLITICS, AND THE INDIVIDUAL

fribbling intervention of mind, or moral, or whatnot. I conceive a man's body as a kind of flame, like a candle flame, forever upright and yet flowing: and the intellect is just the light that is shed on to the things around—which is really mind—but with the mystery of the flame forever flowing, coming God knows how from out of practically nowhere, and being *itself,* whatever there is around it, that it lights up. (*CL*, 180)

This view finds its strongest proponent in Birkin in *Women in Love* and later in the hymns of Don Ramon in *Plumed Serpent*. But like so many of Lawrence's "strongly" held positions, this one too was qualified. In a later letter, Lawrence said that it was impossible for any individual to fulfill his potentiality alone. Blood conscious-ness—a rather subjective, solitary phenomenon—is dependent on the relationship between the sexes: "Because the source of all life and knowledge is in man and woman, and the source of all living is in the interchange and the meeting and mingling of these two: man-life and woman-life, man-knowledge and woman-knowledge, man-being and woman-being" (*CL*, 280).

Between 1913 and 1915, Lawrence moved quickly from one issue to the next. Lawrence wrote about blood consciousness, sex-ual interdependency, and the overall issue of the individual and society. The great social issues of his age provoked most of Law-rence's public and private utterances during the period between the start of *Rainbow* in 1913 and the final draft of *Aaron's Rod* in May 1921: war, revolution, and class struggle. The role of the individual during this volcanic time presented Lawrence with a major source of conflict. Lawrence was more concerned about blood conscious-ness, human sexuality, or the mysterious, nonhuman element in life. His letters reveal this concern quite explicitly.

The Rainbow was written during the first two years of World War I, and Lawrence's reactions to the war in some ways paralleled the thematic conflicts of his novel. Like his heroine, Ursula Brang-wen, Lawrence swung continually between a commitment to other people and to society, and self-commitment. The war polarized all his thoughts about the individual and society. In one letter, for instance, he wrote, "I have never come so near to hating mankind as I am now. They are fools, and vulgar fools, and cowards who will always make a noise beause they are afraid of the silence. I don't even mind if they're killed" (*CL*, 290). But in February 1914, he told Lady Ottoline Morrell: "Let us be good all together, in-stead of just in the privacy of our chambers, let us know the

Society and the Individual 43

intrinsic part of all of us is the best part, the believing part, the passionate, generous part" (*CL*, 311). He hoped that a collective struggle could be waged "for individual freedom and common effort towards good" (*CL*, 311).

This letter is curious because in it Lawrence articulates contradictory concerns. In one paragraph he says, "Let us have *no* personal influence, if possible—not personal magnetism . . . nor persuasion—no 'Follow me'—but only 'Behold!'" In the next he declares, "It is communism based, not on poverty but on riches, not on humility but on pride, not on sacrifice but upon complete fulfillment in the flesh of all strong desire, not in Heaven, but on earth." But then Lawrence makes clear that this communism will work by and for aristocrats: "For the mob shall not crush us nor starve us nor cry us to death. We will deal cunningly with the mob, the greedy soul, we will gradually bring it to subjection" (*CL*, 312). Calling for communism, but just as quickly disassociating it from the mob, was a paradox that did not escape Lawrence. Virtually all of his novels, including *Rainbow*, try to reorder society from stem to stern, though excluding the majority of people. No matter how many times he called for the rule of the masses by a natural aristocracy, Lawrence never carried out this illusion in his fiction. Even in a novel like *Aaron's Rod*, where men like Aaron or Lilly express this ideal, rebellious workers always pop up, demanding to be recognized.

A year after Lawrence's letter to Lady Morrell, Lawrence wrote his own political manifesto to Mary Cannan, hoping to redistribute England's capital. It was as radical as anything the British Communist party would say more than five years later:

> Private ownership of land and industries and means of commerce shall be abolished—then every child born into the world shall have food and clothing and shelter as a birthright, work or no work. A man shall work to earn the things beyond, if he wants them.[. . .] We must form a revolutionary party.[. . .] We must create an idea of a new, freer life, where men and women can really meet on natural terms, instead of being barred within so many barriers.[. . .] Something must be done, and we must begin soon. (*CL*, 322–23)

Nothing in British radical literature, before or after the creation of the Communist party in the early twenties, makes a stronger or more advanced statement about the political reordering of society.

The early years of the war, during which time he wrote *Rain-*

44 CLASS, POLITICS, AND THE INDIVIDUAL

bow, were a period of both optimism and pessimism for Lawrence. During this time he vascillated between extremes: he declared himself for both the primacy of the collective and the absoluteness of the individual. In March 1915, he wrote to Lady Morrell that he wanted to

> set to for the joining together of the multifarious parts, we must knit all words together into a great new utterance, we must cast all personalities into the melting pot, and give a new Humanity its birth. Remember, it is not anything personal we want any more—any of us. It is not honour nor personal satisfaction, it is the incorporation in the great impulse whereby a great people shall come into being, a free race as well as a race of free individuals. (*CL,* 325)

Four months later, in July, shortly before he broke off all correspondence to his friend, Lawrence wrote Bertrand Russell to "drop all your democracy. You must not believe in 'the people.' One class is no better than another.[. . .] There must be an aristocracy of people who have wisdom, and there must be a Ruler: a Kaiser: no Presidents and democracies" (*CL,* 352). The longer the war continued, the wider the gulf grew between Lawrence's interest in participating in a shared effort to transform society, and his distrust for democracy and the masses. This clash is mirrored in *Rainbow,* a book that begins with a profound sense of community and a shared history and ends with Ursula's attempt to reject most social conventions: family, work, and marriage. In the two years it took Lawrence to finish *Rainbow* (March 1913 to March 1915), he went from rejecting individualism as a form of wishful heroics incapable of effecting any social change to a belief in oligarchy.

As the war progressed, Lawrence was less and less able to distinguish between the military and political rulers who were responsible for the war, and the soldiers who fought in it and the relative minority of workers who were initially won over to the war effort in the early years of the fighting. British labor historians like G. D. H. Cole and Standish Meacham report that not only did labor organize against conscription and British military intervention against the Soviet Union after 1917, but that, in fact, immediately before and during the war the labor movement spearheaded most of the social reforms in England. During this time, for example, Cole writes that

> the Labour Movement was practically united in demanding State action for the protection of working-class conditions and for the uplift-

Society and the Individual   45

ing of the bottom dogs. It pressed steadily for the universal application of the legal minimum wage, for the State regulation of hours and conditions of labour through Mines, Factories, and Shop Acts, for a satisfactory system of workmen's compensation, and for an improvement and extension of public education, including school meals and medical treatment as well as inspection.[1]

The Right to Work Bill, sponsored by the unions, called for full employment or, if the state could not provide jobs, "adequate maintenance for all its citizens." A 1918 strike of transport workers called for equal pay for women doing men's work, a unique idea for the times.[2] None of these struggles suggest that money or property were labor's number one priorities.

Lawrence, meanwhile, persisted in his belief that both the ruling and working classes of Britain were "mob-like." In *Rainbow*, the mining town of Wiggiston is described as "grey, dry ash, cold and dead and ugly" (*R*, 63). In the absence of any struggle not seen as a "dark mess," the author often equates a working-class spirit with the working-class landscape. They live in ugliness, and, if you trust the author, their spirit too is broken. Cole, predictably, has a different tale to tell about this period. "The whole mind and temper of the British working class [underwent] a profound change," he wrote, during the years of the First World War:

> Whatever the immediate issues might be, there was a new spirit behind them—a kicking against the pricks of Capitalism, an insistence on the human rights of the worker as a person who was set on "counting" as an individual and refused to be "druv," a capacity for spontaneous mass action which seemed, after the long-sustained orderliness of the Victorian era, something wholly new.[3]

Nevertheless, in response to the war and failure of any popular antiwar resistance with which he could identify, Lawrence seemed to turn his back on his father's class and considered opting for a select few from the upper classes to lead Britain out of its mess. In a July 1915, letter to Russell, he wrote:

> I don't believe in democratic control. I think the working man is fit to elect governors or overseers for his immediate circumstance, but for no more. You must utterly revise the electorate. The working man shall elect superiors for the things that concern him immediately, no more. From the other classes, as they rise, shall be elected the higher governors. The thing must culminate in one real head, as every organic thing

46   CLASS, POLITICS, AND THE INDIVIDUAL

must—no foolish republics with foolish presidents, but an elected King, something like Julius Caesar. And as the men elect and govern the industrial side of life, so the women must elect and govern the domestic side. And there must be a rising rank of women governors, as of men, culminating in a woman Dictator, of equal authority with the supreme Man. It isn's bosh, but rational sense. The whole thing must be living. Above all there must be no democratic control—that is the worst of all. There must be an elected aristocracy. (*CL*, 355–56)

Although this sentiment is more fully expressed in *Women in Love*, *Rainbow* begins to explore the individual's entry into an urban, industrialized society that is contrasted with turn-of-the-century agrarian culture. Lawrence often equated the great leveling process of industrialism—men and women reduced to their lowest common denominators as laborers—with democratic control. The struggle of the individual to realize his full potential despite the ugliness and dreariness of industrial capitalism makes up the essential conflict in *Rainbow*.

The individual in conflict with a changing society is so much a part of the fabric of *Rainbow* that it is puzzling to note how few critics write about the novel without recognizing this fact. Critics either fail, as a rule, to mention any of the effects of social development upon the individual, or they argue that *Rainbow* was Lawrence's great literary effort to create a niche for the individual apart from society. Such a view, shared by an overwhelming number of critics, does not fully account for the extent to which the novel as a whole shows the deep-rootedness of individuals in society: how the family, work, sex, and romance are tied into a social and economic system.

In *Kangaroo*, a novel published eight years after *Rainbow*, Lawrence explained what the rainbow as a symbol meant: "The rainbow was always a sombol to [Somers]—a good symbol: of this peace. A pledge of unbroken faith, between the universe and the innermost" (*K*, 156). Lawrence's own illustration for his novel, a sketch with the inscription, "I have just finished my Rainbow," shows a rainbow arching over the Barger, Walker and Coal Company to a field with stacked wheat. No people at all are shown. Both the passage from *Kangaroo* and the drawing suggest that Lawrence was not interested in escaping society or ignoring its economic base. In fact, he knew he could not. In the novel, the symbol of the rainbow serves in part to locate every character under the umbrella of social and economic realities. The reader is never allowed to forget how tied the individual is to that world.

Society and the Individual

Nowhere else in Lawrence do we have a stronger statement of the conflicts that dominate his works. Given the state of the world in 1914, brought about, Lawrence felt, by an exploitative and bullying political-economic outlook, the individual, Lawrence believed, could survive only as a rebel, by creating a reality of his own. *The Rainbow* is an act of defiance against the materialism of private ownership and the economic and social control over the many by the few—the industrialists, like Tom Brangwen, men without souls.

The Rainbow is deeply rooted in the social facts of English life in the decades preceding the First World War. The early chapters of the book make it clear that Lawrence is critical of what society has become, not its existence per se. Chapter 1 describes the inability of the simple, nonindustrial, pastoral world to fulfill the Brangwen women's imagination and their desire to be more than "blood intimate" with cows, corn, and wheat. The Brangwen woman

> strained her eyes to see what man had done in fighting outwards to knowledge, she strained to hear how he uttered himself in his conquest, her deepest desire hung on the battle that she heard, far off, being waged on the edge of the unknown. She also wanted to know, and to be of the fighting host. (*R*, 3)

Not to be part of this outside, social world would mean not to be fully human. To be more than the "pulsing heat of creation," to wake up from the "drowse of blood intimacy," the women strove to leave the Marsh Farm. Milking cows may have been enough for the Brangwen men, but the women "wanted another form of life than this, something that was not blood-intimacy" (*R*, 3). They wanted ideas, the "spoken word beyond" the farm. The world was changing and so must the people. To "enlarge [one's] own scope and range and freedom" it was necessary to migrate toward the city. Only in the city could Ursula learn her advanced notions about politics, education, women's rights, and colonialism. For Lawrence, the women's insistence on leaving the Marsh Farm for an urban existence was indicative of their strength and imagination.

However, instead of fulfilling these longings, Anna Brangwen's flight from the farm signals the beginning of an unending disintegration for herself, her husband, and their children. Modern industrial capitalism was not set up to satisfy one's creative urgings. Quite the contrary: it functioned primarily to create a profit for a few and misery for virtually everyone else. It also, as Ursula learned, made satisfying interpersonal relationships all but impossible. Physical nature and the fulfillment that derived from their labor had given the Brangwen men a sense of harmony with the world and with themselves, something modern capitalism could never offer. Uprooted from nature and from a small, closely-knit community, alienated from their work, the men cannot survive. Although the women sometimes enjoy a measure of interiority, the men do not, if only because they labor in industry and do not have the time or energy to do so. In their struggle to achieve a bond among themselves and with society, most characters fail. Some, like Tom Brangwen, Ursula's uncle, and Anton Skrebensky, end up serving the machine. Others, like Will and Anna Brangwen, rely on a sensualism that undermines their full development as social as well as private individuals.

The disintegrative force of society is revealed through Lawrence's portrayals of city life, industrialism, organized religion, colonialism, schooling, and the industrial labor force. More often than not, he makes no distinction between those who run the schools and industry and those who are its victims. Schoolmasters are depicted as tyrants, but the children they brutalize are described as rats, thieves, and piteous creatures beyond hope. People with authority are bullies, and most of the people they bully are broken, incapable of changing society. Tom Brangwen, the colliery owner, is marked by "his own dark corruption." Some hope still resides with workers: they are simultaneously vital and dead: "Like creatures with no more hope, but which still live and have passionate being, within some utterly unliving shell, [the miners] passed meaninglessly along, with strange, isolated dignity. It was as if a hard, horny shell enclosed them all" (*R*, 345). Ursula is one notable exception to the leveling quality of industrialism. She is a rebel, who resists every inch of the way the injurious quality of capitalist materialism.

One by one she rejects all social institutions, the mechanisms of an "evil system where she must brutalize herself to live" (*R*, 406). All of England was falling victim to "a blind, sordid, strenuous activity, all for nothing, fuming with dirty smoke and running trains and groping in the bowels of the earth, all for nothing" (*R*, 465). The tangibles of life, which include, for Ursula, most people, are the "old, dead things" (*R*, 461). Recognizing no potential social force or class capable of turning things around, with society di-

Society and the Individual 49

vided into essentially two classes—the bullies and the wretched—Ursula quite logically turns inward.

Lawrence's criticism of prewar British capitalism was sharp and generally accurate. When he relegates everyone but his heroine to the city of the damned and when, at the end of his book, he pictures the "old, brittle corruption of houses and factories," swept away by a revolutionary rainbow, the narrative becomes swamped in mysticism. Nevertheless, no contemporary of Lawrence was more precise in showing how, on the verge of world war, British capitalism destroyed the basis for successful personal relationships within the family and between men and women. At times carried away by the rhetoric of Ursula's denunciations of all things social, the novel returns tirelessly to the facts of social life.

For Lawrence, British capitalism was always in conflict with the individual's aspirations. At virtually every point the individual was thwarted by one or another aspect of urban social life. The city was where men went mad with their hallucinatory, that is, "fixed," ideas about climbing the social ladder. In cities, "the baser material conditions" flourished, encouraging men to pursue their ideas about "nationalism, liberty, science" (R, 254). In the city neither nature nor human relationships flourished—only industry.

The first of the Brangwen women, Lydia Lensky, loses her husband in London where, in exile from Poland, he "lived in a sort of insane irritability," transfixed by the idea of a Polish rebellion against imperial Russia. After Lensky's death, Lydia flees to the countryside where "her soul roused to attention" (R, 47). There she meets and marries Tom Brangwen, thus begetting the first generations of Brangwens who, in their turn, come to regard the city as a nemesis, always interfering with the harmony that nature alone is able to bring.

Lydia's marriage is one of the more successful relationships in *Rainbow*, in part because Lydia and Tom Brangwen are still one generation away from urbanized, industrialized England. The real disintegration of the Brangwen family begins with Anna and Will Brangwen. For Lydia's son-in-law, London is the "ponderous massive, ugly superstructure of a world of man upon a world of nature! It frightened and awed him. The works of men were more terrible than man himself, almost monstrous" (R, 190). The city becomes the symbol for Will, as it does later for his daughter Ursula, of an obstructing social world. Lawrence was undeniably radical in his denunciation of a social system, which repressed

50   CLASS, POLITICS, AND THE INDIVIDUAL

man's feelings and his social relationships. Will's solution, however, was to suggest an impossibility; the return to a preindustrial state. In considering how terrible man's works have become, Will longs for a pristine state, not unlike Ursula's vision at the very end of the novel:

> And yet, for his own part, for his private being, Brangwen felt that the whole of the man's world was exterior and extraneous to his own real life with Anna. Sweep away the whole monstrous superstructure of the world to-day, cities and industries and civilisation, leave only the bare earth with plants growing and waters running, and he would not mind, so long as he were whole, had Anna and the child and the new, strange certainty in his soul. Then, if he were naked, he would find clothing somewhere, he would make a shelter and bring food to his wife (*R*, 190)

Will's feelings are multiplied many times in the next Brangwen generation. Ursula sees that her life and the workers' lives come to a dead end wherever industry is concentrated. When Ursula visits her uncle's colliery in Wiggiston, Yorkshire, she comes to the cul-de-sac of life. Wiggiston represents the antithesis of integrative nature. The colliery and the economic system it stands for are an underworld. The city is inimical to everything that nurtured earlier generations of Brangwens at the Marsh Farm. The workers themselves have become part of the dreadful landscape. They are "not like living people, but like spectres" (*R*, 344). Wiggiston "was like some gruesome dream, some ugly, dead, amorphous mood become concrete" (*R*, 345).

This particular scene is indicative of the complex language Lawrence uses to describe the effects of capitalism. The author's description is a mixture of realism and fiction. If, as Lawrence suggests, capitalism is a bad dream, and one cannot awaken from such a nightmare through social reform, then the solution is to have better dreams—which is precisely what happens at the end of the novel when Ursula has her rainbow vision. Lawrence's own inability to come to grips politically with capitalism is most evident when he drifts from a realistic view of society to a mystical one. In *Rainbow*, Lawrence cannot resolve the contradictions of capitalism because he has no faith in any form of political struggle or political ideology or in the existence of a potentially revolutionary class. Therefore he can give no concrete expression to how things will change.

Lawrence's attack against the "old, dead things" extends beyond

Society and the Individual

urbanism and industrialism. After chapter 5, when Anna Brangwen moves away from the farm, the conflict becomes more intense and pervasive between individuation and the disintegrative forces of society. The closer Anna's daughter, Ursula, gets to contemporary industrial society, the more passionate becomes the individual's fight to remain intact. Whereas earlier Brangwens attempted to define themselves through their work—notably Tom and Will, Ursula's grandfather and father, respectively—Ursula "learned to harden her soul in resistance to and denial of all that was outside her, harden herself upon her own being" (R, 221) By the time Ursula is fifteen, institutions like work and religion, which served her parents and grandparents, fail her miserably. For Ursula, unlike her elders, the primary consideration becomes the self against the world: "—How could one become free? She hated religion, because it lent itself to her confusion. She abused everything. She wanted to become hard, indifferent, brutally callous to everything but just the immediate need, the immediate satisfaction" (R, 286). In contrast to her father, for whom his craft and his belief in the beauty of the cathedral were things he could live by, Ursula's passion was "to know her own maximum self," most of the time in "contradistinction to the rest of life" (R, 301). Will Brangwen often lived through his work, but Ursula finds that work is brutalizing. One by one she rejects the conventions of her parents and grandparents. "She was isolated now from the life of her childhood, a foreigner in a new life, of work and mechanical consideration" (R, 406).

Whether it be college—"a little, slovenly laboratory for the factory, a warehouse of dead unreality" (R, 435)—teaching, or work in industry, the process of socialization is a process of disillusionment and psychic disintegration for Lawrence's characters, though only a few, like Ursula, seem to notice. The more she experiences the world, the more "everything went to produce vulgar things, to encumber material life" (R, 436). Instead of expanding the world for her, education and work reduce it for Ursula, imprisoning her. Paul Morel liberated himself from his parents through work, art, and sex. On the other hand, Ursula seems to discover herself through her childhood rejection of society.

Against the science, rationality, and consciousness of modern capitalism, Ursula counterposes the spiritual, the irrational, and the ineffable. "That which she was, positively, was dark and unrevealed" (R, 437). Unlike Paul Morel, who grew to manhood in a rich social setting, Ursula's development appears to take place in a

52 CLASS, POLITICS, AND THE INDIVIDUAL

dark, spiritual underworld, Lawrence's reaction to a society that had begun to sour in 1914. The concrete, often brutal world of the Morels is put aside here, in its place Lawrence substituted an inner, romanticized world. The conventional, foolish world continued to believe in its science and knowledge, saying that "beyond our light and our order there is nothing," nothing more than our "illuminating consciousness" (*R*, 443). Ursula dares to challenge these premises.

For a time her lover, Anton Skrebensky, tries to inhabit this same inner core of darkness, disregarding society's claim to an "eternal light of knowledge." He ultimately fails because Anton lives more to serve British colonialism and industry than to subvert or circumvent it. He has no vitality of his own. The power he has is not Ursula's power of interiority but the threat over men's lives that a colonial government gives to its officers. Skrebensky is like the younger Tom Brangwen: in the name of money, both men coerce until they themselves are emptied of all life. As part of her final rejection of the social and political status quo, Ursula links the vacuity of her lover with British imperialism:

> You think [she says to Anton] the Indians are simpler than us, and so you'll enjoy being near them and being a lord over them. And you'll feel so righteous, governing them for their own good. Who are you, to feel righteous? What are you, to feel righteous? What are you righteous about in your governing? Your governing stinks. What do you govern for, but to make things there as dead and mean as they are here!
> (*R*, 461)

The Rainbow was kept out of print in England from 1915 to 1926. Although the reason most often heard was that the novel was "a monotonous wilderness of phallicism," as reported by the *London Daily News* on 5 October 1915, statements like Ursula's above must have contributed to the book's unpopularity with the British Morality Council.

By the novel's end, the outside world for Ursula has been replaced by one of her imagination. Having decided that she no longer has any use for people, when her "antagonism to the social imposition was for the time complete and final" (*R*, 450), Ursula becomes "stronger than all the world. The world was not strong—she was strong. The world existed only in a secondary sense:—she existed supremely" (*R*, 452). British civilization was spectral. Using the final image of the rainbow, Ursula begins to embody a

Society and the Individual

wholly new reality. The forces of dead materialism are swept away like husks and shells: "There was a space between [Ursula] and the shell of [civilization]. It was burst, there was a rift in it. Soon she would have her root fixed in a new Day, her nakedness would take itself the bed of a new sky and a new air, this old, decaying, fibrous husk would be gone" (*R*, 492).

Ursula's vision at the book's end does not bear the weight of the many contradictions Lawrence describes throughout his novel: the rainbow image does not truly resolve them. The fact that Lawrence's next novel, *Women in Love*, in part a sequel to *Rainbow*, is still obsessed with the "old, dead things" of capitalist society bears witness to Lawrence's uncertainty about his symbol. As *Rainbow* demonstrates, Ursula's individuality, however necessary to shield her from society, does not necessarily work for anyone else. The elemental, private self that serves Ursula, utterly fails her lover, Anton. In his later works, as in his "Autobiographical Sketch," Lawrence was much sharper on this point: as much as he worried about being taken over by the working class, he wanted to maintain "my passional consciousness and my old blood-affinity with my fellow-men" (*Ph 2*, 596). In *Rainbow*, Lawrence discovered that individuality can be a double-edged sword: it brings a measure of relief to Ursula, but it makes intimate, loving relationships all but impossible.

After chapter 1, no blood affinity exists in *Rainbow*, except among the colliers. *The Rainbow* concentrates on the Brangwen family and not on workers who may, in the final analysis, have much of what Lawrence wanted—passional consciousness and a collective warmth. This focus on the middle and upper classes testifies to Lawrence's distrust of class and class warfare. In July 1915, a few months after the publication of his novel, Lawrence expressed his mistrust of class struggle:

> The war [he wrote to Lady Morrell] is resolving itself into a war between Labour and Capital. Unless real leaders step forward, to lead in the light of a wide-embracing philosophy, there will be another French Revolution muddle. We shall never finish our fight with Germany. The fight will shift to England. And we must be ready *in time* to direct the way, to win the truth. (*CL*, 351)

Part of this fear comes across in both *Rainbow* and in *Women in Love*, where workers are given no active role and are characterized only en masse.

54 CLASS, POLITICS, AND THE INDIVIDUAL

The Rainbow, then, is divided on the value of extreme individuality. Certainly it is the story of successive generations' unsuccessful attempts to secure fulfilling sexual or family relationships. One of the major unresolved themes of the novel is the distinction between positive and negative wills: the positing of one ego against another. Lawrence seemed driven in two directions at once: articulating the need for the individual to work out his own destiny, by and through himself, and showing time after time that man cannot be free from his social as well as personal relations. Lawrence opted for one notion—the self-sufficient individual—and often proved another: the failure of the idealistic view that one could operate in a hermetically sealed world and still maintain satisfactory rapport with someone else. Each generation of male Brangwens tries to dominate his spouse, and each wife or mistress in turn resents this intrusion upon her inner self. The net result, Lawrence proves, is that they all depend upon the people they love.

Beginning with Tom and Lydia Brangwen, couples seem terribly detached from one another, as if achieving one's own selfhood presupposed the rejection of all others. For a time after her marriage, Lydia began to set aside her husband. "She did not want him nor his secrets nor his game, he was deposed, he was cast out" (*R,* 58). At first, like two substances suspended in solution, their lives touch but are never integrated. After years of keeping herself unviolated by society or interpersonal intimacy, Lydia finds that she did not completely know her husband. When he dies in a flood, it is as if she and her daughter Anna are preparing the body of a stranger. Having prized for so long the absoluteness of self, neither wife nor daughter feels much grief at Brangwen's death. The inviolability of the individual soul has made strangers of them all: "I did not know you in life. You are beyond me, supreme now in death," Anna says to the body, "awe-stricken, almost glad" (*R,* 248). Lawrence wished to replace the "pale citizens" of a falsified "social mechanism" with another sort of creature—one rich in darkness, vitality, and selfhood. At the same time, he created individuals unknowable to one another. The schism between men and women expresses Lawrence's contradictory view of individuality: he extolled the supremacy of the individual but then showed how the isolated man or woman was incomplete. The pure states of the self, like the allotropic states of diamond and coal, never merge; nor, in fact, can they coexist. To know one's maximum self, to stay free and undominated, it is often necessary to deny social and personal ties. For Ursula, such a struggle is expressed in trium-

Society and the Individual **55**

phant terms, but no other character can extricate him or herself from society.

The Rainbow experimented with the notion that the maximization of the self in our century is possible only when the individual distances himself from industrial capitalism. The more characters like Winifred, Lensky, and Anton begin to put forward the idea of community—that the individual, from Anton's perspective, "was important in so far as he represented all humanity" (*R*, 327),—the more "a sort of nullity" begins to grip them in their hearts. To be socialized is to die. Ursula's odyssey through society is proof that "the community is an abstraction from the many, and is not the many themselves," when the " 'common good' becomes a general nuisance, representing the vulgar, conservative materialism at a low level" (*R*, 327). Here Lawrence is speaking directly to the reader. When Anton speaks of duty—"to keep in mind the material, the immediate welfare of every man" (*R*, 327), to execute "the better idea of the state" (*R*, 444)—he begins to create a "deadness" around Ursula, "a sterility, as if the world were ashes" (*R*, 314). Skrebensky is, like Tom Brangwen, the worst product of modern capitalism. Tom runs the machines of industry and Skrebensky, a colonialist, makes certain these machines dominate the world.

Ursula's father, Will, matches his daughter in being "perfectly self-contained." Like Ursula, "he was himself, the absolute, the rest of the world was the object that should contribute to his being" (*R*, 225). Yet his self-containment serves to destroy not to cultivate new forms of being. In fact, Will's ego begins to overwhelm his wife's; he tries to bully her and nearly destroys his marriage. Ursula is saved from the hollowness of civilization by her interiority, but this same quality in her father is destructive. In Ursula, selfhood is the soil from which will spring a new generation of individuals, but Will's ego is purely selfish and bullying. To survive her husband's bullying, Anna Brangwen first takes refuge in a mechanical sensuality. With the birth of her four children, "Anna continued in her violent trance of motherhood, always busy, often harassed, but always contained in her trance of motherhood. She seemed to exist in her own violent fruitfulness, and it was as if the sun shone tropically on her" (*R*, 217). For Anna and Will individuality is lived in an uncreative, hypnotic state. What Lawrence says about Anna is fundamentally true for all of the Brangwens: "No responsibility, no sense of duty troubled her. The outside, public life was less than nothing to her, really" (*R*, 217).

By contrast, Ursula may be said to have a creative individuality.

56 CLASS, POLITICS, AND THE INDIVIDUAL

Through her we see how utterly the family, industry, and education have failed to fulfill any human aspiration other than a quick profit. More than any other character she denounces a system based on the rule of money and imperial power. Her ultimate rejection of her lover Anton is based primarily on the fact that he identifies with the class of people Ursula feels is ruining England: the people, says Ursula, who rule "in the name of money" (*R*, 461). She alone in the book is against the "old, dead things" that this monied system stands for, and, of course, only she achieves the rainbow vision at the novel's end. No one but Ursula is able to articulate what Lawrence said in his letter to Lady Cynthia Asquith was the message of *Rainbow:* "the older world is done for, toppling on top of us. . . . There must be a new world" (*CL*, 422). That Ursula's rainbow vision is a curious blend of mysticism and radicalism is indicative of Lawrence's uncertainty over which progressive agent of society to identify with. No class in *Rainbow* is capable of effecting the sort of sweeping social changes Ursula envisages.

By the time Ursula imagines the collapse of the old world, Lawrence has spun a complex web of contradictions. Wanting to escape the horrors of an imperialist, capitalist system, Ursula envisions a world she has no hope of realizing: nothing at all exists from the old world with which to effect the new one. She tries to sever her ties with society, but everything she does and everyone she meets is inextricably implicated in society. Ursula is undoubtedly one of Lawrence's great social rebels, but as his next novel, *Women in Love,* makes clear, a rebelliousness based on extreme individuality, with no social allies, soon begins to sour.

Social Decline and the Individual in *Women in Love*

Unlike *Rainbow*, which took nearly two years to finish, *Women in Love* was completed within seven months; Lawrence worked on it from April to November 1916. It was published privately in 1920 and was Lawrence's only work begun and finished during the First World War. Despite the fact that the war is not mentioned in the novel, *Women in Love* reveals more sharply than his previous works the major thematic conflicts that the fighting impressed upon Lawrence's consciousness.

The longer the war continued, the more convinced Lawrence became that neither personal relationships, nor family, nor love,

Society and the Individual 57

nor community could survive industrialism and imperialism. Any positive unity that might have hitherto existed was being destroyed. On this point Lawrence is unequivocally clear. As he wrote to Constance Garnett a month before he finished *Rainbow:* "I think there is no future for England: only a decline and fall. That is the dreadful and unbearable part of it: to have been born into a decadent era, a decline of life, a collapsing civilisation" (*CL*, 383).

Lawrence is far less sure about the future of the status quo. The problem as always was that once he had eliminated all social classes as forces for a progressive change, he was left with a few stranded individuals, none of whom had any realistic ideas about effecting the radical transformation of society Lawrence wanted. *Women in Love* distinguishes between the vitality of the lower and upper classes, but it makes no political distinctions, that is, neither workers nor owners have any genuine revolutionary potential; both worship at the shrine of the industrial machine. Lawrence was obviously confused as to what direction to take in his next novel, *Women in Love*.

Beginning in April, the month he started *Women in Love*, Lawrence's correspondence is dominated by two complementary thoughts: hatred of the public and the need, in his words, "to withdraw into a very real solitude, and lie low there, hidden, to recover. Then the world gradually ceases to exist, and a new world is discovered, where there are as yet no people" (*CL*, 446). Guided by these negative passions, *Women in Love*, more than any other novel, fails to make a distinction between victim and victimizer. By 1916, Lawrence felt that the war was evidence that ruler and ruled wanted the war, believed in its perpetuation:

> I hate the "public," the "people," "society," [he wrote in April] so much that a madness possesses me when I think of them. I hate democracy so much. It almost kills me. But then, I think that "aristocracy" is just as pernicious, only it is much more dead. They are both evil. But there is nothing else, because everybody is either "the people" or "the Capitalist."
> One must forget, only forget, turn one's eyes from the world: that is all. One must live apart, forgetting, having another world, a world as yet uncreated. (*CL*, 446)

His thoughts were dominated by a wish to see the old world destroyed and "a new order of life" constructed. He had no idea how.

Only when the Russian Revolution of 1917 was successful did

58   CLASS, POLITICS, AND THE INDIVIDUAL

Lawrence begin to express some hope in the future. Starting in May, he wrote a series of letters wherein he expressed a desire to learn Russian, to visit the country that would end the war with Germany and build a new society. One such letter in May 1917, is indicative of his new, though short-lived, hopes:

> Russia is bound to run wrong at the first, but she will pull out all right.—As for me, I sincerely hope she will conclude a separate peace. Anything to end the war.—But tell me what news there *really* is, from Petrograd.—In the meantime, I keep my belief in Russia intact, until such time as am forced to relinquish it: for it is the only country where I can plant my hopes. America is a stink-pot in my nostrils, after having been the land of the future for me. (*CL*, 512)

Two months later he wrote that "Russia seems to me now the positive pole of the world's spiritual energy, and American the negative pole. [. . .] As for England, it is quite hopeless" (*CL*, 516). The irony, of course, is that, like the United States, Russia was soon to dash Lawrence's hopes for a better world. His faith in the revolutionary potential (if not actuality) of workers was so tentative that he was unwilling to commit himself to any long-range political struggle. The protracted war undoubtedly contributed to his deep-rooted pesimism about political ideology, militant mass struggle, and the imposition of rule by any class. All of these sentiments are apparent in Birkin, the main character and Lawrence's spokesman in *Women in Love*.

Women in Love must be understood in light of all the contradictions the prolongation of the war solidified in Lawrence. Generally these conflicts took two forms: a desire to be outside the social world entirely, and an equally compelling desire to fire salvos at the middle class in the hope of changing the world. A second point of tension is Lawrence's disappointment with the working class— in particular, Gerald Crich's colliers—and his continual reference to them as the only class of people who possess even the faintest spark of vitality. In the space of only a few days, sometimes even in the same letter, Lawrence expressed these contrary feelings about himself in relationship to the "social ship." To Katherine Mansfield on 7 January 1916, he wrote, "I've done bothering about the world and people—I've finished." And in the same letter, "I'm not going to struggle and strive with anything any more—go like a thistledown, anywhere, having nothing to do with the world, no connection" (*CL*, 410–11). Two days later, however, he told Lady Ot-

Society and the Individual 59

toline Morrell: "One has only to say to one's soul, be still, and let be what will be. One can do absolutely nothing any more, with one's will. Yet still one can be an open door, or at least an unlatched door, for the new era to come. That is all" (*CL*, 412). Letter after letter, like *Women in Love,* expressed hate for Western civilization and yet fear that it would be abandoned to such men as Tom Brangwen, Anton Skrebensky, Gerald Crich, or Herr Loerke, to the mechanics of British business, politics or culture. Lawrence was antisocial, but primarily this meant he hated the icy mechanicalness of industrialists like Crich, or the muddy waters of spiritual and cultural dissolution that bourgeois artists like Loerke represented. Lawrence described his role as a social rebel in a letter to Lady Morrell in February, two months before he began *Women in Love:*

> I feel quite anti-social, against this social whole as it exists. I wish one could be a pirate or a highwayman in these days. But my way of shooting them with noiseless bullets that explode in their souls, these social people of today, perhaps it is more satisfying. But I feel like an outlaw. All my work is a shot at their very innermost strength, these banded people of today. Let them cease to be. Let them make way for another, fewer, stronger, less cowardly people. (*CL*, 428–29)

Women in Love continues the story of Ursula Brangwen insofar as it completes her rejection of all conventional social attachments begun in the earlier work. The war is never mentioned, but, as Lawrence wrote in the 1919 American edition, he wanted the horrors of the war to be taken for granted in his characters. *Women in Love,* Lawrence wrote to Waldo Frank in July 1917, "actually does contain the results in one's soul of the war: it is purely destructive, not like *The Rainbow,* destructive—consummating" (*CL*, 519). As a reaction to the war and to the failure of European civilization, *Women in Love* dramatizes the disintegration of all the social institutions of the twentieth century: industrialization, political struggle, education, romantic love, and culture. The novel is about a society that ended in the war, and it is about the values and culture that apologized for this society.

The action centers principally around four characters, each of whom represents a social class that Lawrence felt had been an accomplice in the destruction of human potentiality. Gerald Crich is the modern industrialist who has no illusions that his main social function is anything but the maximizing of profits. Unlike his rather hypocritical father, Gerald makes no attempt to befriend

60 CLASS, POLITICS, AND THE INDIVIDUAL

workers or to see them as anything but appendages of the industrial machine. The father "worshipped the highest, the great, sympathetic Godhead of humanity" (*WL*, 207), but the god to whom Gerald prays is Mammon. The three other characters are Birkin—Gerald's friend—and the Brangwen sisters, Ursula and Gudrun.

Rupert Birkin is an intellectual, an inspector of schools who, like Ursula in *Rainbow*, is quick to see that education serves to "imprison within a limited, false set of concepts" (*WL*, 34). He identifies himself and his social role with the class he serves. When the contradiction between "actual sensual being and the vicious mental-deliberate profligacy our lot goes in for" (*WL*, 37) becomes too great, he quits his job, as Ursula did in *Rainbow*. Being far less materially committed to the British economic system than Gerald is, Birkin spends most of the novel in full flight from his "lot" and that of society generally. Like Lawrence, Birkin had everything from which to escape but virtually nothing to accept as an alternative. Birkin is the novel's rebel as well as its antihero, a familiar figure in Lawrence's fiction. He is cultured, intellectual, and middle class, and he rejects everything reminiscent of that class. In the chapter called "The Chair," he and Ursula express their common wish "to be disinherited" of "the beloved past" as well as "the accursed present," to be rid of all traces of "an old base world, a detestable society of man" (*WL*, 348). Sentiments of this sort put him in the company of such other characters as Aaron and Lilly in Lawrence's next novel, *Aaron's Rod*, Somers in *Kangaroo*, Kate in *Plumed Serpent*, and the gamekeeper in the *Chatterley* novels. Like them, Birkin has contradictory needs: he would like to be a free individual—free from a mechanical, democratic state—but at the same time he needs the community of certain men. Birkin and Ursula give away a chair because they feel it represents the furniture of a social system they want no part of. Ursula tells Birkin, "We won't care about *anything*" (*WL*, 354). Like the men who appear in subsequent novels, Birkin is not so sure. Being free is one thing, being without any society is another. "One way of getting rid of everything," Ursula suggests to Birkin, is "to get married." "And one way of accepting the whole world," he replies (*WL*, 354).

The following dialogue then takes place, starting with Birkin's question to Ursula:

> "But we want other people with us, don't we?"
> "Why should we?" she asked.

Society and the Individual   61

"I don't know," he said uneasily. "One has a hankering after a sort of further fellowship."

"But why?" she insisted. "Why should you hanker after other people? Why should you need them?"

"Does it end with just our two selves?" he asked, tense.

"Yes—what more do you want? If anybody likes to come along, let them. But why must you run after them?"

"You see," he said, "I always imagine our being really happy with some few other people—a little freedom with people." (*WL*, 355)

Like the novel itself, this dialogue ends inconclusively. Birkin is forever caught between two poles: absolute freedom from society, which Lawrence recognizes is an illusion, and an unwillingness to participate in any sort of collective change.

When by the last chapter, "Exeunt," the author does try to cut this Gordian knot, the result is a statement of religious idealism similar to that which concludes *Rainbow*. Birkin is mourning the loss of his only friend, Gerald. As he stands over the body, he thinks which way Gerald might have gone to save his life, and what direction he himself must take to save his soul. "Was it any good going south, to Italy? Down the old, old Imperial road?" (*WL*, 469). Having dwelled for so long about man's fate, with what path the individual must follow having rejected society, Lawrence is at an impasse. At this point he all but gives up the struggle for a better world and delivers himself to a transcendent order:

> [Birkin] turned away. Either the heart would break or cease to care. Best cease to care. Whatever the mystery which has brought forth man and the universe, it is a nonhuman mystery, it has its own great ends, man is not the criterion. Best leave it all to the vast, creative, nonhuman mystery. Best strive with oneself only, not with the universe. (*WL*, 469–70)

This is rather sleight-of-hand, coming as it does at the end of a work that rather scrupulously describes characters in terms of their social settings: Beldover, Breadalby, Shortlands, and the café society of the European expatriates. *Women in Love*, like *Rainbow*, attempts at every point to relate the madness of a social and political world to the psychic disintegration of a number of individuals. Lawrence's evocation of a nonhuman mystery—a "timeless creative mystery"—that accounts for the creation, dispersal, and recreation of "utter new races and new species in its own hour, new forms of consciousness, new forms of body, new units of being"

(*WL*, 470), is a deus ex machina way of resolving contradictions, suggesting the need not to get involved in class struggles of any kind.

The Brangwen sisters, the two other principal characters along with Birkin and Gerald, are closest in social class to Lawrence himself. Gudrun lives at home in Beldover with her parents, close to the colliery district. Gudrun's sensibilities toward workers remind us how volatile Lawrence's own reactions were to workers. Gudrun, like Lawrence, has a love-hate relationship with the Beldover miners. She is just as fearful of being overwhelmed by them. On the other hand, many of the qualities that Birkin says he is looking for—spontaneity, a nonmechanical, vital sensuality, and a physical consciousness without the middle class's destructive willfulness—characterize the colliers. Furthermore, as the author must have realized, the colliers who work for the Crich family represent the one class of people who never controlled, benefited from, or eulogized the industrial machine.

Perhaps one passage in *Women in Love* best illustrates this pull toward and away from the working class. In the chapter called "Coal-Dust," Gudrun is observing the miners at rest. She is struck by both the potency and the "intense, dark callousness" of these men. They are the dark voices calling out to Birkin, Ursula, Gudrun, and Gerald. The miners embody what these four people are looking for, but the colliers are too much a challenge for any of them to accept. Gudrun, like the others, dares not get too close:

> Their voices sounded out with strong intonation, and the broad dialect was curiously caressing to the blood. It seemed to envelop Gudrun in a labourer's caress, there was in the whole atmosphere, a resonance of physical men, a glamorous thickness of labour and maleness, surcharged in the air.
> To Gudrun, however, it was potent and half-repulsive. [. . .] Now she realised that this was the world of powerful, underworld men who spent most of their time in the darkness. In their voices she could hear the voluptuous resonance of darkness, the strong, dangerous underworld, mindless, inhuman. They sounded also like strange machines, heavy, oiled. The voluptuousness was like that of machinery, cold and iron. (*WL*, 108)

Perhaps because she herself comes from working people, Gudrun finds her contact with these men to be both bracing and frightening:

Society and the Individual 63

> It was the same every evening when she came home, she seemed to move through a wave of disruptive force, that was given off from the presence of thousands of vigorous, underworld, half-automatised colliers, and which went to the brain and the heart, awaking a fatal desire, and a fatal callousness. (*WL*, 108)

These workers "belonged to another world, they had a strange glamour, their voices were full of an intolerable deep resonance, like a machine's burring, a music more maddening than the sirens' long ago" (*WL*, 109). Lawrence responded very much like Gudrun to this siren call. It enchanted him and it maddened him; above all, he could never completely turn his back on it. Responding to their "intolerable deep resonance," Lawrence returns again and again to the miners in such chapters as "Coal-Dust" and "The Industrial Magnate." Yet he never for long considered that the "other world" to which Birkin and Ursula continually referred and where they wished to be, could be the "strong, dangerous underworld" inhabited by the British worker. The great irony, then, of this book is that Birkin wants what workers may in fact already possess. To put it another way, they have always been denied traditional culture, education, reason, science, intellectualism, materialism, logic, and self-consciousness. The more Birkin tries to jettison his own middle-class proclivities, particularly those of an overly acute mental consciousness, the more he resembles the workers he so despises.

The contrast between the major characters and workers is evident throughout *Women in Love*. When Birkin rails against Hermione's fake passion and her "fixed will," he says, "You want to have things in your power. And why? Because you haven't got any real body, any dark sensual body of life. You have no sensuality. You have only your will and your conceit of consciousness, and your lust for power to know" (*WL*, 35). Hermione, in short, is the antithesis of workers, as Lawrence describes them in *Sons and Lovers* and *Women in Love*. And on at least two occasions, to remind the reader of the contrast between bourgeois and working-class characters, Gerald and Gudrun seem for a moment to exchange social roles with the miners, as if to demonstrate that in the midst of the unfeeling world of industrialism, only the underworld of the workers is still alive. The choice of this couple is evidently ironic, since both disdain the miners, although for different reasons. Gudrun is both repulsed by and attracted to "these ugly,

64   CLASS, POLITICS, AND THE INDIVIDUAL

meaningless people." She hates to be among them in their "defaced countryside," yet she is continually subjecting herself to "the insufferable torture" of their company. Gerald is far less ambivalent about them. Workers are merely "instruments," "just accidents, sporadic little unimportant phenomena" (*WL*, 224). Nevertheless, for just a second, both these characters identify with the people they scorn.

Both scenes occur in the chapter called "Death and Love." Gudrun and Gerald are not yet lovers. When his father dies, Gerald turns to Gudrun to fill a void that neither his work, his numerous lovers, nor his family can fill. As they walk toward her home in Beldover, Gudrun thinks of the colliers who make love under the bridge she and Gerald are crossing:

> Gudrun knew that under this dark and lonely bridge the young colliers stood in the darkness with their sweethearts, in rainy weather. And so she wanted to stand under the bridge with *her* sweetheart, and be kissed under the bridge in the invisible darkness. (*WL*, 322)

Repeatedly in this scene Gudrun compares herself to the colliers' lovers and Gerald—"the master of them all"—to the miners. They do not make love, but the implication is clear: only the world of the miners can provide a setting spontaneous and vital enough to nourish the incipient romance between Gudrun and Gerald, neither of whom has had a satisfying relationship before. On the second occasion, the night of their first love making, Gerald steals into Gudrun's house. He is guided there by neighboring colliers and he himself begins to take on their appearance the longer he tramps through the countryside. In the morning, Gerald gets ready to leave before Gudrun's parents awake. In this scene, Gerald has all but become a collier. As he dresses, Gudrun thinks, "It is like a workman getting up to go to work. And I am like a workman's wife" (*WL*, 341). Away from Shortlands, the Criches' home, Gerald experiences, perhaps for the only time in the novel, a sexual and psychic peace that his own world has always denied him.

These two scenes merely suggest that the world of workers, in all ways "under" that of the middle and upper classes, may be redemptive. Lawrence is not out to prove that the British working class could pull society out of its death throes; far from it. As Gerald extends his control over the mining industry, the militant attitude the workers developed during a previous lockout begins to

Society and the Individual

diminish. By the time Crich is able to reduce his miners "to mere mechanical instruments," they have become pale reflections of their parents' generation. "They accepted the new conditions," the narrator says. "They even got a further satisfaction of them." Part of the despair of *Women in Love* is apparent in Lawrence's portrayal of the inert or even reactionary political role played by labor. The workers become accomplices to the new capitalist way of life:

> There was a new world, a new order, strict, terrible, inhuman, but satisfying in its very destructiveness. The men were satisfied to belong to the great and wonderful machine, even whilst it destroyed them. It was what they wanted. It was the highest that man had produced, the most wonderful and super-human. (*WL*, 223)

The point is not the historical accuracy of the statement—it is almost the opposite of what actually occurred in England during the composition of the novel, particularly among the mining unions—but that it was an inevitable outgrowth of Lawrence's social outlook during this time.

The clearest articulation of this point of view, a dominant theme of *Women in Love,* is found in Lawrence's famous letter to Bertrand Russell in July 1915. His remarks include his opening salvos against democracy, which he always, and mistakenly, equated with industrial capitalism and rule by the mob; ironically, workers are never shown to have political power in any of Lawrence's novels. "Our enemy" is democracy, he begins his letter:

> The idea of giving power to the hands of the working class is *wrong.* The working man must elect the immediate government, of his work, of his district, not the ultimate government of the nation. There must be a body of chosen patricians. (*CL*, 353)

What motivated the exponents of democracy, "what is at the back of all international peace-for-ever and democratic control," Lawrence wrote the following month to Lady Asquith, is to continue "in this state of disintegration wherein each separate little ego is an independent little principality by itself." People like Russell, Lawrence continued, want "to be ultimately a free agent." They want "an outward system of nullity, which they call peace and goodwill, so that in their own souls they can be independent little gods, referred nowhere and to nothing, little mortal Absolutes, secure from question" (*CL*, 360). It is curious that this observation seems to apply, at times quite perfectly, to Birkin and Ursula. Lawrence wanted two things simultaneously that, ultimately, he realized were incompatible: freedom from a system of nullity and a natural aristocracy to replace the present state of disintegration. At the same time, he equally mistrusted the egotism and individualistic absolutism that might result from the severance of all social ties.

This dichotomy of interests is revealed through the characterizations of Birkin and Gerald. As the chapters "Coal-Dust," "Industrial Magnate," and "Rabbit" make clear, Gerald represents an age where mechanical efficiency and the perverse will of a few men triumph over nature and over the majority of men. In "Coal-Dust," Gerald forces a horse up to the tracks while a train is passing. The horse is terrified, but Gerald forces it to submit, just as he bosses his workers and, until his relationship with Gudrun, his mistresses—with mechanical ferocity.

In another chapter, Gerald battles with Bismark, his sister's pet rabbit. Once again, Gerald subdues a force of natural vitality, all the while with a "whitish, electric gleam in his face." In "Industrial Magnate," Lawrence describes how Gerald crushes the once-rebellious colliers. By the time the lockout and the strike have been broken, Gerald is in full control of his industry and his men:

> It was the first great step in undoing, the first great phase of chaos, the substitution of the mechanical principle for the organic, the destruction of the organic purpose, the organic unity, and the subordination of every organic unit to the great mechanical purpose. It was pure organic disintegration and pure mechanical organisation. This is the first and finest state of chaos. (*WL*, 223)

Birkin's profound ambivalence toward Gerald is indicative of Lawrence's own love-hate of the "natural" aristocrats he said should rule society. Birkin is initially physically attracted to Gerald and later repelled by his coldness. Birkin is, perversely, drawn to Gerald who, he thinks, will speed up the disintegration of the system. He is seduced by this modern industrial dictator who has perfected "the first and finest state of chaos." Birkin wants the state to disappear fully, and so Gerald has for him the deadly fascination of a king cobra:

> Birkin thought of Gerald. He was one of those strange white wonderful demons from the north, fulfilled in the destructive frost mystery. And was he fated to pass away in this knowledge, this one process of frost-knowledge, death by perfect cold? Was he a messenger, an omen of the universal dissolution into whiteness and snow? (*WL*, 246–47)

Society and the Individual 67

Birkin's reaction to "the destructive frost mystery" of Gerald illustrates the impasse Lawrence eventually found himself in. In one of the key passages of the novel, Birkin describes how best to answer the threat that Gerald represents:

> There was another way, the way of freedom. There was the paradisal entry into pure, single being, the individual soul taking precedence over love and desire for union, stronger than any pangs of emotion, a lovely state of free proud singleness, which accepted the obligation of the permanent connection with others, and with the other, submits to the yoke and leash of love, but never forfeits its own proud individual singleness, even while it loves and yields (*WL*, 247)

This singleness is also the way of Aaron Sisson and of Reardon Lilly in Lawrence's next novel, *Aaron's Rod*. However, as both novels ultimately reveal, Birkin's "other way" is insufficient to meet the challenge of industrialists like Crich or to satisfy the need, even of individualists like Birkin and Ursula, for community and fellowship.

Neither for Birkin, Aaron, nor Lilly did "the paradisal entry into pure, single being" work. It was impossible, and Lawrence must have known it, as the following dialogue between Ursula and Birkin implies:

> "We must get out," he said. "There's nothing for it but to get out, quick."
> "But where?" she said.
> "I don't know," he said. "We'll just wander about for a bit.[. . .]"
> "But where can one go?" she asked anxiously. "After all, there *is* only the world, and none of it is very distant."
> "Still," he said, "I should like to go with you—nowhere. It would be rather wandering just to nowhere. That's the place to get to— nowhere. One wants to wander away from the world's somewheres, into our own nowhere."
> "You see, my love," she said, "I'm so afraid that while we are the only people, we've got to take the world that's given—because there isn't any other." (*WL*, 307)

The exchange ends inconclusively, as does the novel. But within the context of the work, Lawrence demonstrates that, however profound their intimacy may become, Birkin and Ursula find no satisfaction either in the social world or hiding on top of it—in the Austrian mountains. This "other world," as Ursula calls it, is where all things come to an end for the two couples: Gerald falls asleep in the snow and dies; Gudrun has an affair with Loerke—

68 CLASS, POLITICS, AND THE INDIVIDUAL

"the rock bottom of all life," as Lawrence describes him. For a while Ursula comes to believe that she has achieved a "oneness with Birkin, a oneness which struck deeper notes sounding into the heart of the universe, the heart of reality, where she had never existed before" (*WL*, 400). Ursula believes she is "in her new world of reality." But this reality is just as illusory as was Birkin's "own proud individual singleness." He tells her that to make his life "complete, really happy, I want eternal union with a man too: another kind of love" (*WL*, 472–73).

After their long odyssey toward freedom from society, toward singleness of being, and toward sexual intimacy, Birkin and Ursula are snowed in, away from everything they hated. The penultimate chapter of the book, "Snowed Up," seems to be everything Lawrence said he wanted in a letter he wrote soon after he finished his novel. Saving the "sheer essence of man, the sheer supreme understanding," he said,

> needs a detachment from the masses, it needs a body of pure thought, kept sacred and clean from the herd. It needs *this*, before ever there can be any new earth and new heaven. It needs the sanctity of a mystery, the mystery of the initiation into pure being. And must needs be purely private, preserved inviolate. (*CL*, 520)

Birkin and Ursula seem to have this detachment by the end of the book. But instead of liberating them, their purely private inviolateness has further trapped them. Like Aaron and Lilly, who will articulate many of the same illusions about pure singleness of being, Birkin and Ursula have no recourse but to escape from their "retreat." The last chapter fittingly called "Exeunt," was to become a familiar scene for Lawrence personally and for his next two heroes: Aaron in *Aaron's Rod* and Somers in *Kangaroo.* In a way, Lawrence and his characters were trapped by their rhetoric: they unlearned, in the author's words, "all the social lessons . . . to be unsocial entirely" (*CL*, 525). But they also learned the impossibility of dealing "in single, sheer beings—nothing human, only the star-singleness of paradisal souls" (*CL*, 525). Having burned their social bridges, but simultaneously dissatisfied by their solitariness, Ursula and Birkin are motivated at the end primarily by the need to escape.

Women in Love ends with much the same irresolution as does *Rainbow:* reality and mysticism do battle in the very last sentence. In *Women in Love*, Birkin's idealism is added to the narrator's

Society and the Individual 69

lapses into mysticism. In *Rainbow*, Ursula has a vision in which the "old, brittle corruption of houses and factories [were] swept away," and "the world built up in a living fabric of Truth, fitting to the overarching heaven" (*R*, 495). In *Women in Love*, Ursula and Birkin try to consolidate this vision but fail. Having at great length described the physical vitality of the colliers, and then contrasted them with the cold, swordlike mechanicalness of Gerald Crich, Lawrence retreats from his awareness of class. Neither the industrial magnates nor the middle class—the Pompadour society—has anything to offer. These people believe in nothing, "neither heaven nor earth nor hell." After all their cerebral utterances, none of the four middle-class or upper-class individuals can provide anything better than what the miners already have.

Trusting no class and no collective social action, Lawrence had no effective way of dealing with a world that, in Birkin's words, had gone "completely bad . . . in every way." Not merely was the system of industrialism rotten but, says Birkin, "Humanity itself is dry-rotten, really . . . mankind is a dead tree, covered with fine brilliant galls of people" (*WL*, 118). Nothing social coming out of this system has value. *Women in Love* expresses a rationale for destroying the existing social fabric of man, not rebuilding it. "I am sick of world builders," Lawrence wrote. "I want their world smashed up, not set up—all the world smashed up" (*CL*, 542). Gudrun's despair at the novel's end signals the utter bankruptcy of the dominant classes in *Women in Love:*

> The world was finished now, for her. There was only the inner, individual darkness, sensation within the ego, the obscene religious mystery of ultimate reduction, the mystical frictional activities of diabolic reducing down, disintegrating the vital organic body of life. (*WL*, 443)

Birkin and Ursula barely escape this psychic disintegration. They do only because they still believe in the possibility of a new world. What this world could be, and how it could be achieved, eluded them as it did Lawrence.

Notes

1. G. D. H. Cole, *A Short History of the British Working Class Movement, 1789–1947*, rev. ed. (London: George Allen and Unwin, 1948), p. 307.
2. Ibid., p. 358.
3. Ibid., pp. 348–49.

2

Class Conflict and Reaction: *A Collier's Friday Night, The Widowing of Mrs. Holroyd,* and *Touch and Go*

The subject of Lawrence's first play, *A Collier's Friday Night* (1909), his first major novel, *Sons and Lovers* (1913), the poetry that he began to publish in 1909, and many of his short stories that began to appear in 1914, was the British coal miner. The themes that dominate these works include industrial accidents and deaths, strikes, and domestic quarrels. Of the eight full-length plays Lawrence wrote, five are about miners: *The Widowing of Mrs. Holroyd* (1914), *The Daughter-in-Law* (1912), *The Merry-Go-Round* (1912), *A Collier's Friday Night,* and *Touch and Go* (1920). With the exception of this last play, which is about a strike, these works primarily dramatize the breakup of the colliers' family life. Either industrial deaths or marital woes brought on by drinking or a clash in class values and aspirations between the husband and wife make family life a hardship second only to work in the mines.

Lawrence's early works drew upon British labor struggles and upon his personal knowledge of the miners' domestic plight. The period between 1906 and 1920 included the British General Strike, increasingly bitter class struggle in England, and the war. Reviewing this period, A. L. Morton writes in his class history of England that "no such open class antagonism had been seen in Britain since the time of the Chartists."[1] It was a time of strikes often led by rank and file workers in defiance of their union leadership, a time of class warfare that culminated in the formation of the British Communist party immediately after the First World War.

Class Conflict and Reaction

In most cases, the more militant labor struggles were led by or strengthened by the miners. Morton reports that "as early as 1905 there was an important strike among the miners of South Wales" and that by 1910 the strike had greatly widened to include other miners and industrial workers. By 1912 the first national miners' strike had taken place; this led to the formation of the Triple Alliance—of miners, railwaymen, and transport workers.[2] Although an uneasy truce took place early in the war between labor and business, the Russian Revolution put an end to workers' patriotic and nationalist feelings toward the war effort, particularly during Britain's intervention in Russia. The mood among the working classes of both the Allied and Axis powers was perhaps best characterized by the prime minister at that time, Lloyd George:

> Europe is filled with revolutionary ideas. A feeling not of depression, but of passion and revolt reigns in the breasts of the working class against the conditions that prevailed before the War. The whole existing system, political, social, and economic, is regarded with distrust by the whole population of Europe.[3]

Lawrence was not insensitive to this mood, nor was he ever oblivious to the steady decline in the standard of living of workers in the decades prior to the war. He knew about and articulated the concern of workers that the central cause of the unrest in prewar England involved the following contradiction as described by Morton:

> Thus while profits were rising faster than prices, real wages were decreasing by roughly the same proportion and it was the slow perception of this fact, the realisation of the workers that they were growing poorer just at the time their employers were growing richer, which accounts for the bitterness of the great strike struggles of the early years of the present century.[4]

A Collier's Friday Night and *The Widowing of Mrs. Holroyd* are plays about the effects of this economic schism on collier families. *Touch and Go* is Lawrence's account of one of the great coal strikes that took place continually from 1905 to the outbreak of the war. These three plays illustrate, rather sharply, many of the ambivalences always apparent when Lawrence wrote about workers, their bosses, and political and social struggle.

The Widowing of Mrs. Holroyd was produced by an amateur group near Chester in February 1920, and in London in December

1926. Lawrence refused to attend both these performances and the only other play produced in his lifetime, *David*, in 1927. Neither, apparently, have Lawrence's critics taken his plays very seriously. No critical "trend" exists, because very few critics bother to write about Lawrence's drama. Most seem to share George Becker's rather blunt assertion that "of Lawrence's eight plays there is little to say in commendation. The drama was definitely not his forte. . . . *The Widowing of Mrs. Holroyd* . . . [is] the only one that approaches dramatic power."[5]

Nevertheless, the plays are important because they dramatize Lawrence's lifelong concerns. This is particularly true of *Touch and Go*. Probably nowhere in Lawrence's works can the reader find a more complex set of progressive and reactionary utterances regarding class struggle and how it might be resolved. Taken as a body of work, these plays are important because of the light they shed on Lawrence's other fiction that takes up the same subject: the conflict between labor and capital and the social role of the individual. Furthermore, by the mid-1960s the plays seem to have come into their own, and at least one play a year is currently being produced in England and the United States.

A Collier's Friday Night, Lawrence's earliest play, is in some respects a warm-up to *Sons and Lovers*, published four years later. The uneasy alliance between a harassed miner's wife with her college-educated son against an embittered, drinking collier father is reminiscent of the Morel family. The same tensions are apparent and, as in the novel, the differences in attitudes among members of the family have a class basis. These differences run deep, and part of the artistic strength of this and his other plays is that Lawrence did not grasp after easy solutions. Lawrence was twenty-one when he wrote *A Collier's Friday Night*, and it is remarkable how early in his career he showed a willingness not to provide tidy resolutions for class contradictions.

In this play, Ernest Lambert returns home from college "tired out with study." His father, a miner, cannot sympathize since he comes home "after a hard day's work to folks as 'as never a word to say to 'im, 'as shuts up the minute 'e enters the house a'hates the sight of 'im as soon as 'e comes in th' room" (*CPL*, 482). Like Paul Morel, Ernest is a total stranger in his father's house; even their language keeps them apart: the son is educated and bilingual, and the father speaks only dialect. Ernest comes home talking about French poetry and impressionism, nothing his parents could ever relate to. The father complains that both his children are "turnin'

Class Conflict and Reaction

their noses up" at him, all the while he's supporting them: "What other man would keep his sons doing nothing till they're twenty-two?" (*CPL*, 520). Everyone has a grudge to bear, and they all have a sorry tale to tell: the mother blames the father for excessive drinking and insensitivity to her aspirations for the children. The father blames his family for making him feel like a fool and an outsider. The resulting bitterness becomes such that Ernest says of his father, "I would kill him, if it weren't that I shiver at the thought of touching him" (*CPL*, 522).

A Collier's Friday Night never attempts to resolve the contradictions among mother, father, and children. The play, however, raises a theme that appears repeatedly in the later Lawrence: the class ambition of women and the needling of their worker-husbands. Mrs. Lambert has social aspirations and a certain snobbery toward workers, who appear to be common and complacent by contrast. In refusing to accept her class status, Mrs. Lambert creates an unbearable tension within the household—espousing expectations that cannot be satisfied in a collier's home.

However, the author's sympathies are not clearly with either the husband or wife. The grievances of both are legitimate. As is often the case, the reader is caught in the battle between the male and female characters who represent antagonistic class values. Mr. Lambert is coarse and violent, but his wife is arrogant and turns her children against their father. This 1909 play raises a theme that permeates much of Lawrence: escaping the utter dreariness of working-class life was taken for granted for many of his men and women, but the middle class hardly satisfied one's nonmaterialistic yearnings, as is illustrated by Anabel Wrath. She is Gerald Barlow's mistress in *Touch and Go*. For her the middle and upper class have failed to satisfy her spiritual needs: despite her material well-being, she is dissatisfied. "I feel I want a new way of life," she tells Gerald, "something more dignified, more religious, if you like—anyhow, something *positive*" (*CPL*, 351). *A Collier's Friday Night* only begins to touch on this dilemma. It is difficult not to be in sympathy with the miner Lambert who is a slave to industry: "I should like to see him [his son Ernest] go down th' pit every day! I should like to see him working every day in th' hole. No, he won't dirty his fingers" (*CPL*, 520), he appeals unsuccessfully to his wife. A collier's life is hellish, but the alternative suggested by the son is not, as *A Collier's Friday Night* makes clear, terribly appealing either. Ernest may not be able to discuss impressionist or pre-Raphaelite poetry with his family, but his cultural refinement is not

74 CLASS, POLITICS, AND THE INDIVIDUAL

the alternative to the drudgery of his father. Something else is needed, and at this point Lawrence was not sure what the new "positive" way of life could or should be. *A Collier's Friday Night* illustrates many of the suspicions Lawrence felt toward both the working and middle classes.

The Widowing of Mrs. Holroyd continues a theme expressed in *Sons and Lovers* and *A Collier's Friday Night*—the antagonisms between men and women in the collier household. In this play, written about the time of *Sons and Lovers*, Mrs. Holroyd and her lover talk about escaping the tyrannical husband, a collier. Holroyd, like Morel and Lambert, is a worker who fails his wife and children. Whereas the men find some identity in their labor, this is impossible for the wives who, like the women in *Sons and Lovers* and *Rainbow*, need more than the physical life. As the widow Mrs. Holroyd says of her husband:

> I wanted to be a wife to him. But there's nothing at the bottom of him.[. . .] You can't *get* anywhere with him. There's just his body and nothing else. Nothing that keeps him, no anchor, no roots, nothing satisfying. It's a horrible feeling there is about him, that nothing is safe or permanent—nothing is anything. (*CPL*, 42)

She knows that there must be more to life than the drudgery of labor. Worst of all are the industrial accidents and deaths. In one of the most memorable passages in the play, Holroyd's mother expresses her fears to the wife: "Eh, they'll bring 'im 'ome. I know they will, smashed up an' broke! An' one of my sons they've burned down pit till the flesh dropped off 'im, an' one was shot till 'is shoulder was all of a mosh, an' they brought 'em 'ome to me. An' now there's this" (*CPL*, 50). These works dramatize as well as any other plays in British literature an exploitative industrial system that trapped working-class families, often in ways they could not fully understand.

In *The Widowing of Mrs. Holroyd*, everyone's complaint is justifiable: the wife nags, the husband drinks and bullies, Holroyd feels he is like a dog in the house, and his wife gets no emotional or intellectual support. Although the accusations of one against the other are real enough, such marital badgering is futile. Even when a cave-in kills the husband, thus making possible Mrs. Holroyd's dream to escape the town with her lover and children, nothing really is resolved and no one seems vindicated. None of the characters seem the slightest bit conscious of the social system that vic-

Class Conflict and Reaction 75

timizes them all. But confused as he was about what might replace an exploitative industrialism, Lawrence generally acknowledged the fact that some sort of action was necessary to turn the social ship around or, when he was more radical, to scuttle the ship and start again. These plays show the futility of husband and wife bickering and the enormous economic pressures on the working-class family. *The Widowing of Mrs. Holroyd* ends with no hope in sight; everything seems lost: Mrs. Holroyd is widowed and mourns, guilty she denied her husband. The grandmother keens over the loss of her three sons to the pits. Both she and the wife marvel over the grotesquerie of a death that leaves the miner's body looking so vital. Lawrence implies that the day-to-day lot of a worker—particularly a collier—is really a death-in-life. Only the actual killing brings to the attention of the wife how physically dignified her husband actually is. The horror and futility of working-class life is illustrated by the killing of bodies as well as workers' sensibilities and mental consciousness. As the grandmother washes the body of her dead son, she says, "Eh—and he's fair as a lily. Did you ever see a man with a whiter skin—and flesh as fine as the driven snow. He's beautiful, he is, the lamb. Many's the time I've looked at him and I've felt proud of him, I have. And now he lies here. And such arms on 'im!" (*CPL*, 60).

Exactly these sentiments are articulated by the wife and mother-in-law in the short story, "Odour of Chrysanthemums," written about the same year as the play (1913–14): the workers' physical dignity is invariably robbed by industrial labor, and before they are asphyxiated by industrial accidents, workers are often suffocated at home. They suffer insults during their lifetimes, often at the hands of complaining wives, and they die slowly and horribly at work. Their nakedness in life, in sex, does nothing to bring them closer to their wives. Now in death, as they are being laid out for cleaning and dressing, their nakedness seems even more alien to their wives. Elizabeth, the wife of the dead miner in the short story, looks at her husband's body and thinks that "there had been nothing between them, and yet they had come together, exchanging their nakedness repeatedly. Each time he had taken her they had been two isolated beings, far apart as now" (*CS*, 300). In "Odour of Chrysanthemums," the miner's mother echoes the grandmother in *The Widowing of Mrs. Holroyd:* "White as milk, he is, clear as a twelve-month baby, bless him, the darling! Not a mark on him, clear and white, beautiful as ever a child was made" (*CS*, 300).

76 CLASS, POLITICS, AND THE INDIVIDUAL

A Collier's Friday Night, The Widowing of Mrs. Holroyd, and "Odour of Chrysanthemums" contain an implicit political message: as oppressed as he is at home and on the job the British miner is not one to fight back. He complains and he drinks, but in Lawrence's works he does nothing about his lot. After two years of the war Lawrence distrusted any kind of militant collective action and was not about to show workers fighting back. This fear is captured in a letter he wrote to Lady Morrell in 1915:

> We must go very, very carefully at first. The great serpent to destroy, is the will to Power: the desire for one man to have some dominion over his fellow-men. Let us have *no* personal influence, if possible— nor personal magnetism, as they used to call it, nor persuasion—no "Follow me"—but only "Behold." (*CL,* 312)

And in at least three essays—"Nottingham and the Mining Countryside," "The Miner at Home," and "Autobiographical Fragment," Lawrence indicated that much of the class fight had gone out of the British miner.

Despite these fears and hesitations, Lawrence still believed that no one in England could be or should be saved as an individual qua individual. His social instincts prevailed over his desire to flee the horrors of industrialism; and Lawrence was still loyal to his father's class. In the same letter to Lady Morrell, Lawrence holds out the hope that "we" can make a better future, that "I" is a cause not worth fighting for: "And a man shall not come to save his own soul. Let his soul go to hell. He shall come because he knows that his own soul is not the be-all and the end-all, but that all souls of all things do but compose the body of God, and that God indeed shall *Be*" (*CL,* 312). If his plays up to now have proved the validity of anything, it has been that going alone is suicidal. Lawrence's last play about miners, *Touch and Go,* reflects this awareness. It is a play about workers fighting back, about a strike. Except for the short story "Strike," this play is Lawrence's only work devoted entirely to a class fight and its ramifications on the private lives of its participants.

Touch and Go is as sharp an expression as anything Lawrence wrote about the central contradictions in his own life: his desire to escape the drudgery and mindlessness of his own class and yet the impossibility of siding with the middle or upper classes. The play implies a need for social action but then shows how no social class can provide the necessary solutions for a better society. It is both

Class Conflict and Reaction 77

sympathetic to and scornful of workers. Like the letter to Lady Morrell quoted earlier, the play suggests a communal approach to economic control and ends with a plea for putting power in the hands of the "best men" regardless of class:

> We will be aristocrats, [Lawrence wrote to Lady Morrell], and as wise as the serpent in dealing with the mob. For the mob shall not crush us nor starve us nor cry us to death. We will deal cunningly with the mob, the greedy soul, we will gradually bring it to subjection. (*CL*, 312)

The play, like this letter, is simultaneously progressive and reactionary. *Touch and Go* is an important work because it locates all of the numerous conflicts within Lawrence that made a consistent social outlook impossible. In many respects the play, like the three "leadership" novels Lawrence wrote after the war, attempts to do the impossible: radically alter the system without violating the sanctity of the individual and without relying on the class that stood most to gain from such a transformation—the working class.

Touch and Go suggests that in the political-economic affairs of an industrial system, progress is not best served through class struggle. The play is unambiguous on this point: bosses and workers bully one another, back and forth, as to which side will control property. That neither class can rise above the economic question is a fundamental message of the play. Within six years of the completion of *Touch and Go*, Lawrence had written three major novels—*Aaron's Rod, Kangaroo,* and *Plumed Serpent*—each in turn showing how little revolutionary politics avail. In addition, both in the play and in these novels, workers are generally not fully characterized, and most of the men who mediate between the warring classes are middle class and highly educated. In *Touch and Go* this go-between is Oliver Turton, who clearly speaks for the author when he tells the strikers and the owners at the end, "Can't you see it's no good, either side? It's no mortal use. We might as well all die to-morrow, or to-day, or this minute, as to go on bullying one another. . . . We'd *better* all die" (*CPL*, 383). Lawrence's dismissal of class struggle, articulated by Turton, echoes the elitism, the antidemocratic sentiments, and the social bitterness of the earlier work, *Women in Love.*

Touch and Go opens with a speech by Willie Houghton that introduces a number of complex issues around which the characters battle: nothing changes for the better in the social-economic sphere if force is required, but in the absence of class struggle,

78 CLASS, POLITICS, AND THE INDIVIDUAL

change for the worse is inevitable. Workers will earn less and live more precariously than ever. Willie, for example, harangues the workers for not fighting for better wages and living conditions, for settling for too little. Later he becomes morally outraged when the workers respond too eagerly and want, literally, to fight the bosses—to beat them up. The masters are not giving up a thing without a fight, and Willie tells the men that in the future the Barlows will

> make a number of compounds, such as they keep niggers in in South Africa, and there you'll be kept. And every one of you'll have a little brass collar round his neck, with a number on it. You won't have names any more. And you'll go from the compound to the pit, and from the pit back again to the compound.[. . .] And you'll be the most contented set of men alive.—But you won't be men. You won't even be animals. You'll go from number one to number three thousands, a lot of numbered slaves—a new sort of slaves. (*CPL*, 325–26)

The implicit racism here raises an ideological problem in Lawrence's works. Racist epithets are often used to discredit a character, and, on occasion, Lawrence uses racial analogies to apply to the British working class. People of color, he writes, are slavish—in their blood. They do not rebel. What they have in sensuality is nullified by a mindlessness and lack of intellectual or psychic vitality. Sentiments of this kind are found particularly in *Kangaroo*, *Plumed Serpent*, and *Reflections on the Death of a Porcupine*. In *Kangaroo*, for example, the "socialist" Willie Struthers, the reactionary Kangaroo, and Somers, the narrator, customarily use Africans and Asians to express their contempt for people who are apathetic or who wish to be enslaved. Somers says, "The niggers the same. The real sense of liberty only goes with white blood" (*K*, 88). Somers at this point is articulating Diggers's fascist position, but it is also true that no antiracist sentiment is expressed in the novel. The issue of racism is a complex one in Lawrence's work. Given his thoughts about collection action, Lawrence found himself in a dilemma in *Touch and Go*. Workers are "niggers" when they do not fight back and bullies when they do. Lawrence cannot endorse class struggle, but he also shows how workers are victimized and that passivity is suicidal. As his letters and this play make clear, Lawrence desired radical social change, even revolutionary change. But by ending with a plea against action, he guaranteed that his play would end irresolutely.

This debate over the possibility and nature of political, social,

Class Conflict and Reaction

and economic change is the "touch and go" concern of the play. It is examined both in the social arena of the strike through the relationship of the workers to the boss, and in the personal sphere of Gerald Barlow's long affair with Anabel. Since Gerald tries to dominate both the mines and his mistress, the connection between private and social concerns is also addressed. Although by the play's end, Gerald tells the workers he would like to see the system changed "as much as ever you do," he never, in fact, changes, either as a boss or a lover. When Gerald sees that Anabel has developed into a more mellow person, he is more resentful than encouraged. Since he regards himself as perpetually warring against his workers—"to be bullied over trifles is a sign of criminal weakness," Gerald says—he does not look kindly upon the differences he sees in his former lover. "You're sort of softer and sweeter—I'm not sure whether it isn't a touch of Father in you. There's a little sanctified smudge on your face. Are you really a bit sanctified?" When she replies that she is different because she wants "a new way of life—something more dignified, more religious," Gerald shows how little capable or desirous he is of changing: "I think I liked you better before," he tells her. "I don't think I like you with this touch of aureole. People seem to me so horribly self-satisfied when they get a change of heart—they take such a fearful lot of credit to themselves on the strength of it." "Do you feel no different, Gerald?" Anabel asks. "Radically, I can't say I do.—I feel very much more indifferent." "What to?" "Everything," he answers (*CPL*, 351).

Gerald Barlow, the mine owner in *Touch and Go*, is a prototype of Gerald Crich in *Women in Love*. Barlow has introduced modern machinery into the mines, thus speeding up production and greatly increasing profits. Unlike his father, who took a benevolent view of the colliers, Gerald is the new capitalist. Profits come first under his leadership. The older Barlow is hesitant to make the necessary changes, but "it had to be done," he tells Anabel, Gerald's mistress. The system is now "running at top speed, utterly dehumanized, inhuman," Barlow says. Like the miners in *Women in Love*, the colliers in the play are pictured as worn, gloomy, and hollow as a result. "They are a great grief to me. . . . There is something wrong in the quietness, something unnatural. I feel it is unnatural; I feel afraid of it. And I cannot help feeling guilty," the father concludes (*CPL*, 349). Whereas the older man was "sort of crucified on an idea of working people," Gerald has no guilt about exploiting them even further. By this point in the play, Lawrence

80 CLASS, POLITICS, AND THE INDIVIDUAL

seemed to be saying two things: the economic system is ruinous and needs radical change; and workers were more alive during the great lockout and the strike that followed. By the conclusion of the play, however, both these points get lost in Oliver's words of caution to the strikers and to the owners that coercion from either side is equally wrong.

Of the owners, Gerald and his mothers are totally uncompromising and unashamed about their class interests. Compared to the workers' spokesmen—Willie Houghton, an old socialist, and Job Arthur Freer, the local union secretary—Gerald and Mrs. Barlow are attractive because they act decisively and confidently. Willie, who has "preached socialism in the marketplace for thirty years," is so passive that when the workers finally do strike and threaten physical violence, his fondness for workers' control is quickly replaced by a stronger belief in nonviolence. Just before he is stomped by the strikers, Willie tells them: "if you're going to start killing the masters to set yourselves up for bosses—why, kill me along with the masters. For I'd rather die with somebody who has one tiny little spark of decency left—though it is a little tiny spark—than live to triumph with those that have none" (*CPL*, 378). Only the striking workers themselves who remain anonymous and have no major characters to speak for them are ready to win at any cost. The other union leader—Job Arthur—shares Willie's no-win outlook. The local union secretary needs to be physically kicked around the stage by Gerald before he vows revenge. Since, however, the revenge is largely personal and not political, class violence is thoroughly repudiated by the play as a whole. The only character who acts militantly and yet remains appealing is Gerald Barlow, the mine owner.

Lawrence never seems to be able to locate his sympathies in this play. The workers no doubt have been wronged by the mine owners, but nothing looks worse in this play than the unruly mob, especially because their only aim is to redistribute property; they have no higher social aspirations. Lawrence was clearly against physical violence: it reminded him too strongly of the war and of the personal abuse he and his family suffered at the hands of his father. Nor was he particularly attracted to mass movements per se: as a collective, the strikers lack inner vitality, the private strength that Mrs. Barlow calls "the power to be alone." Although their strength is only in their numbers, in their ability to strike, the workers are faulted for always being heard as one voice.

In *Touch and Go*, only Gerald and his mother offer and accept

Class Conflict and Reaction 81

no quarter. They welcome a good fight because it indicates to them that in their blood they are warriors. Lawrence believed in this blood vitality, and every character but Mrs. Barlow and her son snivels or cringes at one time or another during the play. She blames the workers for every indignity the Barlows have suffered:

> Fight, Gerald. You have my blood in you, thank God. Fight for it, Gerald. Spend it as if it were costly, Gerald, drop by drop. Let no dogs lap it.—Look at your father. He set his heart on a plate at the door for the poorest mongrel to eat up. See him now, wasted and crossed out like a mistake—and swear, Gerald, swear to be true to my blood in you. Never lie down during the mob, Gerald. Fight it and stab it, and die fighting. It's a lost hope—but fight. (*CPL*, 341–42)

No other speech in the play carries with it as much conviction or more of Lawrence's elitism. The so-called "blood" vitality is passed along from boss to boss, not from worker to worker, at least in this play. In this passage Lawrence is also commenting on the hypocrisy of the elder Barlow, who is similar to the older Crich in *Women in Love.* In both cases the masters thought they could be friends with the men while the constabulary took shots at the striking miners. Despite the lockout, the strike, and the shooting of two miners by the army, Barlow still harbors illusions about a "family" of shared economic interests between workers and owners. Barlow tells Oliver:

> Privately, I like to think even to this day they bear me no malice, that they have some lingering regard for me. But the master stands before the human being, and the condition of war overrides individuals—they hate the master, even whilst, as a human being he would be their friend. I recognize the inevitable justice. It is the price one has to pay. (*CPL*, 348)

This smug self-righteousness Lawrence could not tolerate. Better the bosses acknowledge they were in a fight to the death with the workers than ask the workers to accept charity while they were being locked out or shot at.

But one of the main issues of the play is that everyone—strikers and management—is guilty of bullying, of trying to get the other side to submit. Mrs. Barlow bullies the workers, just as she imposes her will upon her son and husband. Gerald attempts to boss everyone else, including his mistress, Anabel Wrath. Oliver Turton, Gerald's friend who has no material stake in the outcome of

82 CLASS, POLITICS, AND THE INDIVIDUAL

the strike (in fact, he is the only character who does not seem to work at all), speaks for Lawrence when he tells the strikers:

> Can't you see that it takes two to make a quarrel? And as long as each party hangs on to its own end of the stick, and struggles to get full hold of the stick, the quarrel will continue.[. . .] We're all human beings, after all. And why can't we try really to leave off struggling against one another and set up a new state of things? (*CPL,* 384)

Class struggle and political coercion are not the answers to economic and social hardship. Genuine progress will occur, the play suggests, when the state is taken over by a few honest men who have nothing personal to gain by taking control of the government. As Oliver says at the play's conclusion: "As for power, somebody must have it, you know. It only rests with you to put it into the hands of the best men, the men you *really* believe in.—And as for money, it's life, it's living that matters, not simply having money" (*CPL,* 384).

No other work of Lawrence's fiction reflects sharper divisions in his political and social thinking. The play is radical in the sense that it calls for changes that go far beyond economic ones; most everyone agrees that the current economic system is obsolete and that "a new state of things" is desirable. Yet *Touch and Go* may be Lawrence's only fiction in which the boss—in this case, Gerald—is every bit as radical as the workers, and a good deal more articulate about it: "Look here!" he chides the strikers. "I'm quite as tired of my way of life as you are of yours. If you make me believe you want something better, then I assure you I do: I want what you want. . . . You choose leaders whom I respect, and I'll respect you, do you see?" (*CPL,* 385). And it is Gerald who says "we ought to be able to alter the whole system."

By being critical of the workers, who are pictured as pushy and short-sighted, interested only in a greater share of the wealth, and by portraying Gerald as complex and dynamic, Lawrence suggested that a solution to social ills might be found in such benevolent masters as Gerald or intellectuals like Oliver. The two spokesmen for the workers—Job Arthur and Willie Houghton—can hardly claim anyone's allegiance, especially that of the strikers. In calling upon an enlightened natural aristocracy to lead the miners and owners together to a better future, *Touch and Go* is reminiscent of the way Dickens's novels, in which many labor disputes

Class Conflict and Reaction

figure. In commenting on *Hard Times*, George Bernard Shaw makes an observation that is partially applicable to the author of *Touch and Go:*

> It is especially important to notice that Dickens expressly says in [*Hard Times*] that the workers were wrong to organize themselves in trade unions.[. . .] he turns his back frankly on Democracy, and adopts the idealized Toryism of Carlyle and Ruskin, in which the aristocracy are the masters and superiors of the people, and also the servants of the people and of god. [. . .]
>
> And to this Dickens sticks for the rest of his life. [. . .] he appeals again and again to the governing classes, asking them with every device of reproach, invective, sarcasm, and ridicule of which he is master, what they have to say to this or that evil which it is their professed business to amend or avoid. Nowhere does he appeal to the working classes to take their fate into their own hands and try the democratic plan.[6]

In *Touch and Go,* though not in Lawrence's subsequent works, at least two of Shaw's observations apply. "We're all human beings, after all," Oliver tells the strikers. "And why can't we try really to leave off struggling against one another?" "If you want what is natural and good," he continues, "I'm sure the owners would soon agree with you" (*CPL,* 385). Since the workers throughout the play speak in one rather rowdy voice, it is clear that the few chosen leaders will come not from them but from a more articulate, educated class—the owners. The *First Lady Chatterley,* in fact, is the only work in which Lawrence hints that workers might take their fate into their own hands, without benefit of benevolent, natural aristocrats.

In 1921, a year after *Touch and Go* was published, Lawrence wrote a high school text, *Movements in European History.* Much of this "history" is actually concerned about the future of European civilization, and, ideologically, it parallels the play. What we need is not political coercion, the book argues, but a volitional submission to "some natural, pulsing nobleness." The epilogue of *Movements* deals with the period following the Russian Revolution, when revolutionary struggles and class strife were intensifying throughout Europe. It bothered Lawrence greatly that workers were taking to the streets in Italy—the country he had escaped to in 1920—so he ended his history with this statement, one that is directly applicable to the play:

> There is nothing to be done, *en masse.* But every youth, every girl can make the great historical change inside himself and herself, to care supremely for nothing but the spark of *noblesse* that is in him and in her, and to follow only the leader who is a star of the new, *natural Noblesse.* (*M*, 321)

Gerald Barlow himself is too arrogant and too defiant to fit this description, but he alone has the prerequisite qualities of strength, vitality, and social consciousness. Political elitism as a substitute for collective struggle becomes an important theme throughout Lawrence's works.

Touch and Go, as its name implies, ends uncertainly. The solution to the stalemate between the striking miners and clerks and the masters cannot be left to either side because worker and boss are too blinded by narrow economic considerations. Oliver, who has no economic roots and therefore no apparent class prejudice, is left to mediate. Everyone agrees with or is silenced by Oliver, but no one can see how his utopian system will come to pass. The strike continues, therefore, and the play ends. Gerald, as usual, has the last word, "Now, then, step out of the way." Characters touch for a moment, agree that miners and owners alike are hurt by industrialism and class warfare, and then depart with all their old class hatreds. *Touch and Go* is typical of many of Lawrence's works like *Lost Girl, Women in Love,* and *Lady Chatterley's Lover* where Lawrence acknowledged that class antagonisms cannot be separated from capitalism without some sort of revolution; but, he argued, unless the latter is achieved intellectually and by common consent, the fight will take us around in a circle. Class rule, like sexual bullying, is simply coercion.

Touch and Go attempts to prove that political action plays by the old rules of force and therefore can not be effective. Neither class can move society forward, so only declassed types like Oliver Turton, Birkin in *Women in Love,* Aaron or Lilly in *Aaron's Rod,* Somers in *Kangaroo,* or Mellors in *Lady Chatterley's Lover* can understand that saving souls and selfhood is more important than building unions and fighting for collective aims. As Mrs. Barlow says, in the spirit of these other Lawrentian heroes, "I hate the people. Between my race and them is war—between them and me, between them and my children—for ever war, for ever and ever" (*CPL*, 341). This is precisely how Aaron viewed the agitating communist workers in Italy and how Somers regarded the socialist and fascist forces he saw in Australia.

Class Conflict and Reaction   85

But these works tell more than any one character does. Lawrence is under no illusion that his lack of faith in political or class struggles is itself a solution to the social unhappiness of his men and women. From the lost girl, Alvina, to Mellors, in *Lady Chatterley's Lover,* character after character has to move on, to keep on the move to escape certain stubborn social political realities. Lawrence is enough of a realist in *Touch and Go* to show that no one, certainly none of the strikers, accepts Oliver's pitch; miners and owners are all part of one quarrelsome family.

As such, *Touch and Go* resembles Lawrence's next full-length work, *Aaron's Rod.* In this novel, the main characters, Aaron and Lilly, have nothing positive to say about workers, especially the more militant ones who continually cross their path. They go so far as to argue that, in Oliver's words, "It's the people that are wrong. They want the system much more than the rich do—because they are much more anxious to be rich—never having been rich, poor devils" (*CPL,* 347). Yet in both the novel and in the play, the only potential force of change is represented by the workers; in the play they are striking in support of the clerks—not merely for higher wages for themselves—and in the novel they are in a near-insurrectional struggle for greater political control. Three of the play's main spokesmen—Willie Houghton, Oliver Turton, and Gerald Barlow—all seem to agree on one point: the working man is incapable of bringing about social change. Willie tells the men they "like sinking in—you don't have to stand on your own feet then" (*CPL,* 325). Gerald says to Job Arthur, "I have absolutely no belief in the power of Labour even to bring about anything so positive as bloodshed," and all the union leader can reply is, "I don't know about that—I don't know.—Well" (*CPL,* 362). Oliver, closest to Lawrence, remarks to Gerald, "It seems to me [the British working man] is in nearly as bad a way as the British employer: he's nearly as much beside the point" (*CPL,* 363). But despite these messages, the play says a great deal more.

As *Sons and Lovers, Rainbow,* and *Women in Love* demonstrate, the social setting of Lawrence's works tells its own tale. The background of *Touch and Go* is a strike, and the workers rough up Willie, Oliver, and Gerald in the course of it. For a while the workers, not the owners or the intellectuals like Oliver, call all the shots: they prove the impossibility of management's *not* heeding their demands. When the miners beat up Gerald, only Anabel's intercession makes them release him; no one is permitted the luxury of a purely private life. The play documents the history of the

Barlow family—a family whose story parallels that of industrial England in the post-Victorian era—and proves that as the economic system changes, and the relationship of one class to another is vastly altered, nothing remains the same. *Touch and Go* is about social as well as personal change.

The Barlows's transformation from wealthy farmers to modern industrialists is part of that history. The other is the strike and the lockout, which greatly intensified British labor struggles. Although Barlow is quick to recognize industrial progress, that is, a radical increase in production and in his profits, neither he nor his son can imagine that workers understand in whose interest this progress is operating or at whose expense. Barlow says that "the men of this generation are not like my men. They are worn and gloomy; they have a hollow look that I can't bear to see," and Gerald thinks the men have "no *life* intelligence. The owners may have little enough, but Labour has none. They're just mechanical little things that can make one or two motions, and they're done. They've no more idea of life than a lawn-mower has" (*CPL,* 361). Despite such cynicism, *Touch and Go* chronicles a moment of unambiguous historical and personal change, most of it attributable to the conflict between capital and labor. As both the play and *Women in Love* illustrate, industrialism in the modern period has effected vast changes: increased production and greater power for the capitalists, as well as intensified class hatred. The contradiction in the Barlows's attitude toward the workers is evident: class hatred and worker apathy cannot exist simultaneously. They cannot be the bullies everyone calls them and still lack, in Gerald's words, "either energy or the courage or the bit of necessary passion, or slap-dash" to smash things up (*CPL,* 361).

"An artist is usually a damned liar, but his art, if it be art, will tell you the truth of his day," Lawrence wrote in his *Studies of Classic American Literature.* As much as any work, this play illustrates the schism that exists between Gerald's or Oliver's "adorning moral" and the direction the play takes. Job Arthur, Gerald, and Oliver may believe that workers and owners share a common economic interest. Gerald tells the miners that he is in need as much as they of "a new way of life," and Job Arthur refers to the coal pits as "the cow that gives the milk. . . . I don't want to kill the cow and share up the meat. It's like killing the goose that laid the golden egg. I want to keep the cow healthy and strong" (*CPL,* 328). All this implies that workers and bosses share a common interest in developing a more equitable economic and political system. No doubt, one of Lawrence's aims was to promote class unity. During

Class Conflict and Reaction 87

the war he wrote many letters to this effect: head off class warfare by emphasizing what the British had in common. In one such letter he wrote to Lady Morrell:

> To live, we must all unite, and bring all the knowledge into a coherent whole, we must all set to for the joining together of the multifarious parts, we must knit all words together into a great new utterance, we must call all personalities into the melting pot, and give a new Humanity its birth. (*CL*, 325)

And in a later letter to Lady Asquith, he wrote that "Prime Ministers and Capitalists and artisans all working in pure effort towards God—here, tomorrow, in this England" could bring to pass a better future, one in which "there will be love enough" (*CL*, 343).

But as *Touch and Go* and the correspondence make clear, Lawrence must have known this was wishful thinking. On 29 May 1915, eleven days after his letter to Lady Asquith, Lawrence put aside for the moment his vision of England as a melting pot: "As for political revolution," he wrote to Russell, "that too must come. . . . We shall have to sound the resurrection soon" (*CL*, 346). The action of the play demonstrates that all the talk about class unity solved nothing. The miners in *Touch and Go*—like the miners in *Women in Love*—appear to be enjoying neither the goose nor the eggs. The notion that both classes have an equal stake in the maintenance or even the reform of a more benevolent form of capitalism produces only one result in this play: universal dissatisfaction. The end of the play is rather like its beginning: nothing has changed for the workers or bosses and no one is happy. The passion developed during the course of the work is not universal love or brotherhood but the very thing Lawrence feared most—class hatred. This is the real source of the energy of such characters as Job Arthur, Gerald, Mrs. Barlow, and the chorus of miners. The great activity and energy of *Touch and Go* is stage center—where the strike is taking place. The last scene of the play provides a suitable frame for the opening scene: Gerald stalks offstage with nothing more to say, and the colliers still dominate the town's marketplace.

Notes

1. A. L. Morton, *A People's History of England* (London: Lawrence and Wishart, 1945), p. 493.
2. Ibid., pp. 494–95.

3. As quoted in ibid., p. 520.
4. Ibid., p. 493.
5. George Becker, *D. H. Lawrence* (New York: Frederick Ungar, 1980), p. 18.
6. George Bernard Shaw, *Introduction to Hard Times* (New York: W. W. Norton, 1966), p. 338.

3

Revolution and Retreat: *Aaron's Rod, Kangaroo,* and *Plumed Serpent*

Aaron's Rod: Political Action, Private Escape

In Europe during the 1920s, the central ideological battles were fought between various stripes of socialism and communism on the one hand, and reaction—fascism—on the other. During the first five years of this decade, Lawrence produced three novels: *Aaron's Rod* (1922), *Kangaroo* (1923), and *Plumed Serpent* (1925). Despite the author's insistence that political idealism was "the real enemy today . . . this enemy incarnate," the three books express their own political sentiments and biases. Each of these works kept pace with the social struggles both in England and in Europe. The foremost of these was the war, whose horrors for Lawrence cast shadows over *Aaron's Rod* and *Kangaroo.* These three so-called leadership novels are complex works because they attempt to do at least two things at once: move away from the trauma of politics as Lawrence had experienced it and acknowledge that the age was an intensely political one; politics could not be ignored without paying a heavy psychological price.

Aaron's Rod was written the same year Lawrence wrote his psychoanalytic text, *Fantasia of the Unconscious,* a work concerned with the same topics as the novel: war, the need for both individual freedom and social leadership, man's capacity to be free, and Lawrence's growing view that real freedom for most men came from a sort of voluntary submission. *Fantasia* expressed ideas and emotions that paralleled those of the novels. Lawrence's statement on

90 CLASS, POLITICS, AND THE INDIVIDUAL

education might have been one of Rawdon Lilly's monologues in *Aaron's Rod:*

> First and foremost establish a rule over [boys], a proud, harsh, manly rule. Make them *know* that at every moment they are in the shadow of a proud, strong, adult authority.[. . .] The leaders must stand for life, and they must not ask the simple followers to point out the direction. When the leaders assume responsibility they relieve the followers forever of the burden of finding a way. Relieved of his hateful incubus of responsibility for general affairs, the populace can again become free and happy and spontaneous, leaving matters to their superiors. No newspapers—the mass of people never learning to read. The evolving once more of the great spontaneous gestures of life. (*PF*, 123)

This sentiment figured very heavily in Lawrence's three major postwar novels. In anguish over the war, Lawrence formulated his own utopia in *Fantasia,* one in which "men have got to choose their leaders, and obey them to the death. And it must be a system of culminating aristocracy, society tapering like a pyramid to the supreme leader" (*PF*, 210). By the end of each of the novels, Lawrence discovered he could not mix soldiering and unquestioning obedience with freedom; soldiers who are also individuals and not pieces of a machine do not exist. In *Kangaroo,* Harriet tells Somers that the people were not being allowed to choose their leaders; Somers was choosing for them. Lawrence wanted antithetical things, and his novels show that he himself was unhappily aware of this fact.

Aaron's Rod, in particular, articulates two contrary notions. In part, the novel explains why the individual must "fulfill his own soul" and "every woman must be herself, herself only, not some man's instrument, or some embodied theory" (*AR*, 347). As a reaction to the war, to the mounting strikes in England, and to the socialist and fascist movements in Italy, *Aaron's Rod* stressed that "your own single oneness is your destiny." Yet most of the last chapter is given over to Lilly's theory of leadership: "The woman must submit, but deeply, deeply submit" to man. And, he concludes "men must submit to the greater soul in a man, for their guidance: and women must submit to the positive power-soul in man, for their being" (*AR*, 347).

The Plumed Serpent is also an exploratory work. This novel opens with an attack on socialist politics for being overly concerned with material reform. The Mexican Indians are pictured as caught between capitalism on the right and the political revolutionaries on the left: "These flat Indians," the narrator says, "were

Revolution and Retreat   91

symbols in the great script of modern socialism, they were figures
of the pathos of the victims of modern industry and capitalism.
That was all they were used for: symbols in the weary script of
socialism and anarchy" (*PS,* 54). At the same time, Lawrence was
not satisfied that Aaron's or Lilly's rejection of social struggle was
a sufficient response to the postwar decline of Western civilization.
In his forward to *Fantasia,* Lawrence wrote that we must live by a
vision, a set of beliefs, or we will perish. It is impossible for man to
survive through wholly individualistic yearnings:

> And finally, it seems to me that even art is utterly dependent on
> philosophy: or if you prefer it, on a metaphysic. The metaphysic or
> philosophy may not be anywhere very accurately stated and may be
> quite unconscious, in the artist, yet it is a metaphysic that governs men
> at the time, and is by all men more or less comprehended and lived.
> Men live and see according to some gradually developing and gradually
> withering vision. This vision exists also as a dynamic idea or metaphy-
> sic—exists first as such. Then it is unfolded into life and art. (*PF,* 57)

"We have no future; neither for our hopes nor our aims nor our
art. It has all gone gray and opaque." What we need now, Lawrence concluded, was a new vision "put down in terms of belief
and of knowledge. And then go forward again, to the fulfillment in
life and art" (*PF,* 57). These three novels are an utterance of a new
vision for mankind, just as they are an attempt to show that conventional political practices could not work.

The political visionaries of Lawrence's time all seemed to be
coercive. During and after the war, Lawrence spoke continually
against repression of any sort. In *Sons and Lovers,* for example, he
had described the terrible effects of a bullying father upon his
family. In *Rainbow,* he showed how British education intimidated
and crushed the spirits of teachers and students. By becoming an
agent of British imperialism, Anton Skrebensky had become dehumanized. In *Rainbow* and in its sequel, *Women in Love,* Lawrence portrayed colliers as the victims of an industrial system that
beat all life out of people. In *Movements in European History,* he
attempted to prove that 1920 socialism in Italy meant that "we,"
the middle and intellectual class, "began to be bullied every way."
Socialism "was all pure bullying. And this was socialism. After all,
I, who am not a workman, why should I be bullied by workmen?
Because bullying is what it amounts to" (*M,* 316). As usual, however, Lawrence's fiction simultaneously argues very nearly the opposite point of view about political coercion.

Lawrence feared politics because he hated the notion that the individual could be manipulated by the economic and political forces beyond his control. Political bullying, his novels show, starts with the capitalist class but continues when ordinary working-class people force themselves upon such free spirits as Aaron, Lilly, or Somers—characters with whom Lawrence at least partially identified. The three novels initially establish the abstract values of freedom and self-expression. They then turn to the leaders who will, presumably, oversee this state of freedom that the masses themselves are unable to handle. Finally, however, the works question both the notion of individual freedom and the possibility of honest political leadership. Aaron is not convinced by Lilly's insistence that most men must submit to "some greater soul than theirs." Somers recoils from submitting to Kangaroo, and Kate Leslie in *Plumed Serpent* is very cautious about her marriage to Cipriano; she is equally tentative about her association to Cipriano's nationalist movement. In all three novels, Lawrence was experimenting with these conflicting notions: man must be freed from political compulsions; most men could not be left to their own devices and therefore had to be led; but political control, even by such "natural aristocrats" as Don Ramon and General Cipriano, led to the corruption of power. Except for Kate Leslie, who stays for the time being in Mexico, the protagonists of *Aaron's Rod* and *Kangaroo* find themselves torn between the desire to belong and the desire to be free from social commitment. Like many of Lawrence's heroes, they have little choice but to move on. The leadership novels reveal a strong attraction for and a deep mistrust of "the leader who is a star of the new, *natural Noblesse.*"

After World War I, Lawrence was pulled in two directions. He repeatedly articulated his desire to put everything social and political behind him. He wanted to escape the aftermath of the war, which included an intensifying class struggle throughout Europe. At the same time he was combative and longed for real social change. He told a friend that he had escaped across the English Channel because "England is a mud-bathos" (*CL*, 645). The year *Aaron's Rod* was published he wrote, "If I knew how to, I'd really join myself to the revolutionary socialists now. I think the time has come for a real struggle. That's the only thing I care for: the death struggle (*CL*, 639). Lawrence pictured his heroes Aaron and Lilly escaping the oppression of class, politics, family, and romance, but by the time they reach Italy, they have encountered everything they left behind. In a letter to Earl Brewster, Lawrence wrote that Aaron was "misbehaving and putting ten fingers to his nose at

Revolution and Retreat

everything" (*CL*, 653). But the novel makes it clear that such iconoclasm in the absence of any social involvement only leads to a dead end. In *Aaron's Rod* and *Kangaroo*, the sense that all activity has led to an impasse is compounded by Lawrence's general insistence that one political movement is like any other: all social ideologies end up looking alike. *The Plumed Serpent*, in fact, was an attempt to project a vision—at various times, sexual, religious, and mystical—that would obviate class struggle altogether.

Yet for all the mysiticism and subjectivity that the main characters in these novels evoke, the works portray social and political settings in rich detail. Much more is present than the single-minded individuality of a Lilly, Somers, or Kate. Their private utterances never eclipse the descriptions of society in Italy, Australia, or Mexico. Georg Lukács described "a relation between the artist and the outer world," a relation many modern writers try to deny. Lukács's ideas are useful in showing how Lawrence's works move far ahead of the characters, who wish to sever their connections with the social world. Lukács explained that Lawrence and his contemporaries imposed on their subject matter " a certain level of generalization": "Whether he will or no, every writer describes the condition of mankind. The present social condition of mankind is at the root of even the most abstract, the most solipsistic vision of the future."[1] The modernist sensibility was, argued Lukács, characterized by extreme subjectivism, where reality was seen as fundamentally static, and social development was rejected out of hand. In the early decades of the twentieth century, Lukács wrote, "a new feature in the later stages in this process is the increasing exclusiveness, the radical, almost brutal elimination of social significance."[2] Elements of this elimination are apparent in Lawrence's three novels. Aaron and Lilly react to what they see as "the awful gulfing whirlpool of horror in the social life" and therefore reject any social commitment. Cooley in *Kangaroo* and Don Ramon in *Plumed Serpent* lead movements whose slogans are those of religious mysticism. Nevertheless, Lawrence was satisfied neither by his heroes' explicit rejection of society and politics, nor by their avowal of mysticism as a solution to capitalism and war.

The subject of these novels is the effect of twentieth-century politics upon the individual. But in concentrating upon the potential of select individuals, Lawrence recreated the old class snobbery—the sort he professed to hate. For example, in *Aaron's Rod*, Lilly argued that any fixed set of ideas was apt to be false. "You thought," he tells Aaron, "there was something outside, to justify

94 CLASS, POLITICS, AND THE INDIVIDUAL

you: God, or a creed, or a prescription. But remember, your soul inside you is your only Godhead" (*AR*, 344). But Lawrence's faith in the individual only extended to a few. *Aaron's Rod* begins to bring into focus what later *Kangaroo* and *Plumed Serpent* make explicit: the majority of people need to submit to their betters. Women should submit willingly and lovingly to men, and workers should submit to their natural superiors. Between Lilly's theory of natural male dominance over women and his prejudicial statements—for example, "the flea-bitten Asiatics . . . teem by the billion. Higher types breed slower" (*AR*, 113), Lawrence left himself open to charges of fascism. Whereas Lilly's statements go much further than anything Lawrence wrote in his own voice—for example, his essay called "Aristocracy" in *Reflections on the Death of a Porcupine*—no character in *Aaron's Rod* challenges Lilly's elitism in any way.

During the early 1920s when Lawrence wrote these novels, he never clearly denounced the growth of European fascism. At times he identified with it. Both the authoritarianism and mysticism of *Plumed Serpent* seem commensurate with certain manifestations of fascism, particularly with the sort of material Lawrence's friend Rolf Gardiner was turning out in the middle and late twenties. For a while, Lawrence was attracted to Gardiner's interest in myth, cultural and blood consciousness, and the idea of voluntary submission. Certainly not every criticism of industrialism, capitalism, or even of Western imperialism, came from the left in the 1920s. As John Harrison pointed out in his book *The Reactionaries,* a number of writers, Lawrence included, became critics of democracy because they believed that the masses needed to be ruled by superior individuals. Lawrence's occasional and indiscriminate attacks on reason, science, the intellect, and democracy, as well as his elevation of various "natural aristocrats," drew him, at least for a time, to more doctrinaire fascists. Lawrence was susceptible to charges that he was an inchoate fascist because he always failed to distinguish between the failures of bourgeois democracy and the perniciousness of fascism. As Mary Freeman wrote in her study of Lawrence, his "condemnation of fascism was no more vehement than his condemnation of our Christian-capitalist culture."[3]

In *Rainbow*, Lawrence attacked Western democracy, which he saw as controlled by big business and administered by a class more concerned with money and property than with the well-being of the individual. But he was not interested in democracy, increased

Revolution and Retreat

participation of the citizenry, or a greater distribution of property or political power. The real menace to what Lawrence regarded as the free human spirit was not the strong-armed type—like Cooley or Don Ramon—but the people themselves, whom Lilly referred to as "the infinite crowds of howling savages outside there in the unspeakable" (*AR*, 58). In the "Nightmare" chapter of *Kangaroo*, Lawrence all but blames the British people for World War 1.

Aaron's Rod, like *Women in Love*, was begun during the war and, unlike the earlier work, provides a running commentary on the war and its political and social effects. Both novels have spokesmen who, at least partially, speak for Lawrence. In *Aaron's Rod*, Rawdon Lilly and Aaron Sisson argue what Lawrence himself wrote in his essays, notably "Education of the People" (1918), "The Reality of Peace" (1917), and "Democracy" (1916, revised in 1920), all written about the time of the novel. However, for all the book's statements about the necessity of preserving the individual soul, it is steeped in the history and class struggle of Europe during the period immediately after the First World War, a fact that is often overlooked. The most striking feature of *Aaron's Rod* is that it does not cleave to a fixed idea. Like the other two "leadership novels," this book is quite unsure about itself, very much in doubt as to its message.

Aaron's Rod is a fascinating book insofar as it is transitional among Lawrence's works. It begins a trio of books that are largely exploratory, concerned with the question of political involvement and Lawrence's ambivalent desire to become part of a mass struggle for social reform. But *Aaron's Rod* also ends a period. "It is the last of my serious English novels—the end of *The Rainbow*, *Women in Love* line. It had to be written—and had to come to such an end."[4] These two books do not contain large political movements such as the socialist and fascist street fights portrayed in *Aaron's Rod* or in *Kangaroo*. To fully identify Lawrence with Lilly or Aaron is to miss the point that the novel drifts about in theme and in sequence of events because, as Lawrence wrote in 1921, "I don't feel very sure about anything" (*CL*, 665). *Aaron's Rod* is accurate enough in its portrayal of postwar Europe, its disillusioned, aimless middle class, and the contending fascist and socialist movements. The novel can hardly be termed doctrinaire in any real sense. When Lilly holds forth on the absoluteness of the individual, saying that "every man is a sacred and holy individual, *never* to be violated" (*AR*, 328), Lawrence introduces the bombing

96   CLASS, POLITICS, AND THE INDIVIDUAL

incident that destroys Aaron's flute. The passage also destroys, rather abruptly, the absurdity of asserting the inviolability of the individual in the middle of a civil insurrection. This scene alone shows how much distance Lawrence put between himself and his major characters, despite his sympathy for them. *Aaron's Rod* is a more complex work than many of Lawrence's readers may have given him credit for.

Thematically, *Aaron's Rod* closely resembles its predecessors, *Rainbow* and *Women in Love*. Ursula and Birkin's voices are often echoed by Aaron Sisson and Rawdon Lilly. If anything, *Aaron's Rod*, as a post-mortem of Europe after the First World War, is an even more end-of-the-world examination of Western civilization. In *Women in Love*, Birkin and Ursula did sustain an intimate, if turbulent relationship. In *Aaron's Rod*, the only real show of love is between two men, Aaron and Lilly, and they are about to separate as the novel ends. The principal male characters of these two works share a common bitterness and anguish at the British Empire, which they see as life threatening. However, although Birkin is often ridiculed by Hermione and Ursula, Lawrence speaks through him in a far steadier voice than he does through either Lilly and Aaron. The frequent misanthropic statements in *Aaron's Rod* are not so confidently reported, and Lawrence does not wholly identify with either character. Throughout their European pilgrimage, Aaron and Lilly meet various women, fellow intellectuals, and veterans who are not ready to accept their notions of extreme isolation and elitism. Lilly's angst mostly appears as an anomaly, a trait not shared by the other expatriates. *Aaron's Rod* says many of the same things as its predecessor, but it lacks the center that Birkin provides in *Women in Love*.

The book begins with many of the same premises as *Rainbow* and *Women in Love*. The first is that bourgeois artists, men who become expatriates like Aaron and Lilly, with a certain amount of money, no social or family ties, and an open-ended European itinerary, have one major responsibility: "simply, pure self-possession." For people such as Ursula, Birkin, Aaron, and Lilly, man's real crime is his denial of his own singleness. One of the principal illusions that *Aaron's Rod* ends up debunking is expressed when Aaron rationalizes his desertion of his wife and children:

> He realized that he had never intended to yield himself fully to her or to anything: that he did not intend ever to yield himself up entirely to

Revolution and Retreat

> her or to anything: that his very being pivoted on the fact of his isolate self-responsibility, aloneness. His intrinsic and central aloneness was the very centre of his being. (*AR*, 191)

It is easy to understand where this sentiment comes from: years of failed materialism in the name of political struggles, war, and revolution. Since, as Aaron and Lilly come to believe, the great horrors fo the twentieth century have been committed in the name of various idealisms, one must reject false gods. "There is no goal outside you," Lilly tells Aaron. "There is no goal. I loathe goals more than any other impertinence. Gaols, they are. Bah—jails and jailers, gaols and gaolers—" (*AR*, 338).

Lawrence wanted very much to believe that "loneliness and singleness as a fulfilment a state of fulfilment" (*AR*, 195) was possible, but his novel proved he could not sustain this hope. Both men prove throughout the book how dependent they are on the kindness and tolerance of others; Aaron's life is saved by the patient and loving care he gets from his would-be misanthropic friend Lilly. As for Aaron's flute playing and Lilly's writing, both would be impossible without the patronage they receive from the aristocratic British expatriates they have repudiated. Lawrence's portrayal of Aaron and Lilly reflects his yearning to be apart from political struggles and coercion. At the same time, Lawrence realized that men, in fact, depend upon one another on a variety of levels.

A conflict exists, therefore, between the world as perceived by Aaron and Lilly and the wider world as it is revealed in the action of the novel. The utterances of Aaron, especially, attempt to prove that despite family, friends, love affairs, and politics, one may exist "without any moral necessity or any other necessity." For example, after a brief affair with the Marchesa, Aaron senses that he has had "just a glimpse" of the freedom he is seeking: "Outside—they had got outside the castle of so-called human life. Outside the horrible, stinking human castle of life. A bit of true, limpid freedom" (*AR*, 267). Aaron is momentarily caught up in "the blessedness of being alone in the universe." Aaron's flute partially symbolizes this private escape from social responsibility. At its best, rarefied art can transport man "beyond this dank and beastly dungeon of feelings and moral necessity" (*AR*, 267). Aaron's music has this quality, which, Lawrence shows in a key scene, cannot last forever. In the socially tumultuous world of Europe in the 1920s, Aaron's rod is fragile indeed.

98   CLASS, POLITICS, AND THE INDIVIDUAL

Immediately after this scene, where Aaron plays his flute for the Marchesa, creating a music that carries them "outside the horrible, stinking human castle of life," an anarchist or socialist throws a bomb. To Lawrence, most organized politics were a form of terror, and this act of terrorism is an occasion for him to remind the reader that those creative individuals like Aaron or Lilly who think they can charm the world with their art are cruelly mistaken; they themselves may, in fact, be the worst sort of idealists. The world will not be transported or put to sleep. But Lawrence is also making a political statement of his own.

Those who most intrude upon the artistic and dynamic individual—men like Lilly and Aaron—are ultimately not the wealthy, the industrialists, or even the politicians. In *Aaron's Rod*, the outsiders seem to be the people themselves, in this case, the Italian workers who, after the war, are on the verge of a socialist or fascist revolution. They are the bullies, the ones who throw the bombs and rob Aaron as he walks among a group of soldiers. They create a "sudden gulf, the awful gulfing whirlpool of horror in the social life" (*AR*, 329). When the bomb is thrown, Lilly supposes it was thrown by an anarchist. "It's all the same," Aaron replies. One group is as destructive as the next. Aaron's rod is destroyed in the attack, and as the two men throw the rod into the river, Lilly observes that "it's an end." Like the last line in *Plumed Serpent*, Lilly's statement is deliberately ambiguous. The destroyed flute is an end to idealisms of all sorts, particularly those of the would-be artist in isolation. The broken rod is also an acknowledgment that we live in a world torn by class strike. Castles in the sky cannot be brought to earth, least of all through art alone. But as Lawrence and the novel go on to picture a better world, the end of Aaron's rod is also a new start. "It'll grow again," Lilly tells Aaron. "It's a reed, a water-plant—you can't kill it" (*AR*, 331).

Political turmoil, an important theme, is never resolved. Politics, like Aaron's personal life, is anarchistic, and this is part of Lawrence's design. The welter of events in the novel is a result of Lawrence's various interpretations of class in the social order. For one thing, Lawrence continually equated the ideas of democracy with that of the bourgeois-dominated, capitalist West. As a result, in *Aaron's Rod* history was rather crudely fictionalized. Europe was not pictured as an oligarchic society but, rather, one of ochlocratic rule. Government was not shown as run by this or that parliamentary party, representing the major industrialists of the time, but by the "voice of the Herd [. . .] which is vulgar, com-

Revolution and Retreat

mon, ugly, like the voice of the man in the crowd" (*M*, 312). Political power, according to *Aaron's Rod*, is in the hands of the mob, which, Lilly explains, has power over "the nation, Lloyd George and Northcliffe and the police and money" (*AR*, 112). Had workers such power, it is not clear why the workers and soldiers in this novel are in a constant state of rebellion. Lawrence does not account for the violent struggles that do take place in *Aaron's Rod* by both the left- and right-wing forces.

The paramount battle being waged here, however, is the survival of individualists and artists like Lilly and Aaron within the hostile environment of a politically crazed society. Most of the time these men seem motivated by a sentiment repeated like a refrain by Lilly throughout the novel:

> Why, I'll tell you the real truth. I think every man is a sacred and holy individual, *never* to be violated. I think there is only one think I hate to the verge of madness, and that is *bullying*. To see any living creature *bullied*, in *any* way, almost makes a murderer of me. That is true. (*AR*, 328)

Neither Aaron nor Lilly is willing to identify with a social class. Aaron, for example, leaves his job as secretary to the Miners Union because of its "silly wrangling". One sort of social bullying is no different from any other. No particular distinction is made, for example, between the bullies in government and the rebellious workers in the streets. But *Aaron's Rod* proves that it is impossible to write history and politics without taking a class position, even if that position is in flux. As often as Lilly and Aaron agree that "everything is so awful—so dismal and dreary" (*AR*, 75), some things, and especially certain groups of people, are less awful and dismal than others. *Aaron's Rod*, in particular, is indicative of the difficulty Lawrence had in denouncing politics without making a political statement, though he often reversed that position later. When, for example, Aaron tries to run away from his own class, he becomes for a while a lapdog for various Italian and British aristocrats from whom he takes lodgings, money, and women. While neither Lilly nor Aaron is enamored of his hosts, their real mistrust is of the radicalized workers and exsoldiers who roam the streets. All the hands-on violence—Aaron's robbery, his destroyed flute, and the terrorist bombs—is done by workers; they are the bullies in this book. Revolutionary violence is identified with mugging and wanton hooliganism.

100   CLASS, POLITICS, AND THE INDIVIDUAL

Perhaps what most discredited Lawrence's insistence that social or political bullying injured the human spirit was his racial stereotyping. In one notable monologue to the sleeping Aaron, Lilly sounds like Somers and Cooley in *Kangaroo* and Kate Leslie in *Plumed Serpent* as he describes his hatred of certain races. For all his iconoclasm, Lilly appears to have accepted the racism of his age with little reservation:

> I can't do with folk who teem by the billion, like the Chinese and Japs and orientals altogether. Only vermin teem by the billion. Higher types breed slower. I would have loved them Aztecs and the Red Indians. I *know* they hold the element in life which I am looking for— they had living pride. Not like the flea-bitten Asiatics—even niggers are better than Asiatics, though they are wallowers—the American races—and the South Sea Islanders—the Marquesans, the Maori blood. That was the true blood. It wasn't frightened. (*AR*, 113)

This is delivered to the sleeping Aaron, and so no response is forthcoming. Yet what Lilly says is not so different from the way Lawrence has pictured the teeming masses, at one point "the power of evil" that "had got" Aaron. There is a logic to Lilly's words if one assumes the world is divided between the craven, swarming multitudes, and those few who possess in Lilly's words, "the dark, living, fructifying power." In his portrayal of the Italian workers, the recently discharged soldiers, and nonwhites gener-ally, Lawrence was, to use an expression from his essay "Morality and the Novel," putting his "thumb in the scale." In this essay, Lawrence took to task those writers who allowed their own biases to get in the way of things as they are. "Life is so made that opposites sway about a trembling centre of balance," he wrote. The novel should reflect this delicate balance:

> The novel is the highest example of subtle inter-relatedness that man has discovered. Everything is true in its own time, place, circumstance, and untrue outside of its own place, time, circumstance. If you try to nail anything down, in the novel, either it kills the novel, or the novel gets up and walks away with the nail.
> Morality in the novel is the trembling instability of the balance. When the novelist puts his thumb in the scale, to pull down the balance to his own predilection, that is immorality. (*Ph 1*, 528)

This balance is more difficult to find in *Aaron's Rod* than it is in his previous works. Like *Kangaroo*, the earlier novel is shadowed by the war, and the nightmare for Lawrence was far from over. The

Revolution and Retreat

tone of almost total alienation from anything social is set in the first paragraph: "The War was over, and there was a sense of relief that was almost a new menace. A man felt the violence of the nightmare released into the general air." This generalized atmosphere of violence and unrest permeates the novel. We may take Lilly and Aaron's dread of the war and its release of class violence in Europe as Lawrence's own. The author makes this position explicit in *Movements in European History*, published one year before the novel in 1921. Virtually all the monologues in *Aaron's Rod* reflect Lawrence's suspicion of any social commitment. Beginning with *Sons and Lovers*, Lawrence's great theme was social and personal coercion. In this early novel, the constraints of society as a whole were mirrored in the aspect of a bullying father. Especially during the war years and after, Lawrence made unsuccessful attempts to clear out altogether from the social and political ship. In *Aaron's Rod*, for example, even a combination of two people is one too many, as Lilly tells Aaron: "And can you find two men to stick together, without feeling criminal, and without cringing, and without betraying one another? You can't" (*AR*, 118). The last two lines of the novel echo this desperate urge to be free once and for all of any ties: "And whom shall I submit to?" Aaron asks his friend. "You soul will tell you," Lilly replies. Yet even while Lilly is hectoring Aaron abut the need to be a free soul, he is writing a prescription for the inevitability of human ties, regardless of their quality.

Lawrence never really succeeded in cutting himself or his characters off from society or political struggle. He repeatedly wrote in his essays that he never wanted to. In "Morality and the Novel," he described this fierce attachment to life outside himself:

> If we think about it, we find that our life *consists in* this achieving of a pure relationship between ourselves and the living universe about us. This is how I "save my soul" by accomplishing a pure relationship between me and another person, me and other people, me and a nation, me and a race of men, me and the animals [. . .] an infinity of pure relations, big and little. [. . .] This, if we knew it, is our life and our eternity: the subtle, perfected relation between me and my whole circumambient universe. (*Ph 1*, 528)

Unfortunately, the relationships that emerge in *Aaron's Rod* are among the most bitter in Lawrence's works. The book began as an experiment, from the desire to start a new future after the ruins of war: "Let there be clean and pure division first, perfected sin-

102   CLASS, POLITICS, AND THE INDIVIDUAL

gleness," the narrator says. "That is the only way to final, living unison: through sheer, finished singleness" (*AR,* 150). Because Lawrence neither really wanted such singleness, nor thought it existed in a social world, these sentiments quickly and terribly turned into their opposite. Beginning with Lilly's racial, class, and sexual theories, *Aaron's Rod* often becomes a justification for women's submission to men, workers to political leaders, and for certain races to other races. Although an occasional minor character may jeer at these pronouncements, no opposing major voice is heard.

Nevertheless, by the time the anarchist's bomb is thrown during Lilly's soliloquy on the sacredness and holiness of the individual and his freedom, Lawrence is well aware of the danger of identifying too closely with his main characters: the irony is not lost on Lawrence that preaching absolute individuality in the middle of a social upheaval is wishful thinking at best and destructive idealism at worst. Lawrence moved away from Lilly and Aaron in other respects as well. The novel begins with Aaron walking away from his class, his family, and his responsibilities as a union organizer. He became immediately attracted to Lilly's rejection of romantic love, domesticity, and participation in what Lilly felt was an antiquated mode of social life. The men share the assumption that certain men—themselves—could ignore the social and political movements of the day and proceed to carve out a wholly private state. Then as events unfold, Lawrence proves the utter futility of these illusions.

To start with, Lilly and Aaron develop a relationship that is, at times, sexual. Aaron, who at the start of the novel curdles "with revulsion as from something foul" at the thought of goodwill, spends the middle section of the novel following Lilly around Europe. When Aaron becomes ill, Lilly administers to him as to a child or lover:

> Quickly [Lilly] uncovered the blond lower body of his patient, and began to rub the abdomen with oil, using a slow rhythmic, curculating motion, a sort of massage. For a long time he rubbed finely and steadily, then went over the whole of the lower body, mindless, as if in a sort of incantation. He rubbed every speck of the man's lower body—the abdomen, the buttocks, the thighs and knees, down to the feet, rubbed it all warm and glowing with camphorated oil, every bit of it, chafing the toes swiftly, till he was almost exhausted. (*AR,* 112)

The scene is significant for various reasons. It illustrates the extent to which Lawrence was aware of the irony of first Aaron's, then

Revolution and Retreat 103

Lilly's posturing that, as the latter puts it, "You learn to be quite alone, and possess your own soul in isolation." No one in *Aaron's Rod* is ever alone for too long. Aaron's various short-lived affairs and his devotion to his music also show how much these characters need an intimate, sensual relationship with the world around them. The times that Aaron is making love or playing music demonstrate his desire to establish direct, intense connections with others. None of these things have much in common with his boast to "let there be clean and pure division . . . perfected through singleness." Ironically, this ability to establish a direct, uncomplicated, and often sensual relationship with people and with nature is a phenomenon Lawrence most often identified with workers. Aaron has this quality. Lilly, a writer with no roots in the working class, is far less capable of making these connections; he seems to come to life only through Aaron. Lawrence named two of his chapters "Pillar of Salt." At least one of these pillars refers to the notion that the "loud hoarse noise of humanity" could or should be ignored.

During the course of his travels throughout Italy, Aaron is caught in the middle of street fighting between the carabinieri and various gangs of ex-soldiers, fascists, and socialists. Although politically and temperamentally Lawrence is disdainful of them all, his descriptive languages does discriminate between the social classes. The rich are variously described as birdlike, colorless, grotesquely shaped, and bleached. And although in regard to workers he is often insulting, Lawrence invariably ascribes to them a vitality that is clearly missing among the English and Italian aristocrats. The fear and occasional loathing that Aaron feels toward the rioting workers is unlike the profound sense he has that his wealthy hosts are all but dead in spirit and that their civilization is clearly in decay. Having overtly rejected political partisanship, Lawrence does, in fact, point to distinct class characteristics that do not favor the propertied classes. For Aaron, to be among the European nobility with their military and intellectual friends is to be among ghosts:

> Lady Franks, Sir William, all the guests, they talked and manoeuvered with their visible personalities, manipulating the masks of themselves. And underneath there was something invisible and dying—something fading, wilting; the essential plasm of themselves: their invisible being. (*AR*, 192)

While the peasants, soldiers, and workers may be rioting in the streets, the class that Sir William represents—as well as his middle-

104 CLASS, POLITICS, AND THE INDIVIDUAL

class guests and hangers-on—has strength only to drink, talk about the war and culture, and, generally, to reduce the world to a set of abstractions. In all respects, men like Sir William are not quite as alive as the Italian workers who, if nothing else, are warriors:

> There was something frightening in their lean, strong Italian jaws, something inhuman and possessed-looking in their foreign, southern-shaped faces, so much more formed and demon-looking than northern faces. They had a demon-like set purpose, and the noise of their voices was like a jarring of steel weapons. (*AR*, 215)

Certainly Lawrence is of two minds here: these workers are dangerous, but at least they manifest a vital energy. Contrast this with the description of Sir William, a man who no longer has anything to offer society:

> Sir William lifted his glass with an odd little smirk, some touch of a strange, prim old satyr lurking in his oddly inclined head. Nay, more than satyr: that curious, rather terrible iron demon that has fought with the world and wrung wealth from it, and which knows all about it. The devilish spirit of iron itself, and iron machines. So, with his strange, old smile showing his teeth rather terribly, the old knight glowered sightlessly over his glass at Aaron. (*AR*, 199)

For long sections in the novel, scenes oscillate between descriptions of the aristocratic and bourgeois classes and of Italian workers. At one point in his travels, Aaron meets two English gentlemen, Francis Dekker and Angus Guest. Both independently wealthy, they are off to Rome to paint, "not yet" to earn a living by it. The way Lawrence portrays them, as well as Aaron's subsequent ride in a third-class carriage of an Italian train, is indicative of Lawrence's sensitivity to class differences and his appraisal of these contrasts. The Englishmen, one a war hero and the other a former official in the British War Office, are foppish; one looks like a "white owl . . . like some bird-like creature." They are "two weird young birds." They drink and wonder why the war has so badly affected the liqueurs, the quality of food, restaurant and hotel service, and the state of the arts. They insist that Aaron travel first class with them to Rome but he cannot afford to do so. Once he is in third class he takes stock of the other passengers, who contrast sharply with Dekker and Guest, "the flower of civilisation and the salt of the earth, namely, young, well-to-do Englishmen":

Revolution and Retreat

> Here in the third class carriage, there was no tight string around every man. They were not all trussed with self-conscious string as tight as capons. They had a sufficient amount of callousness and indifference and natural equanimity. True, one of them spat continually on the floor, in large spits. And another sat with his boots all unlaced and his collar off, and various important buttons undone. They did not seem to care if bits of themselves did show, through the gaps in the wrapping. Aaron winced—but he preferred it to English tightness. He was pleased, he was happy with the Italians. He thought how generous and natural they were. (*AR*, 234)

If intellectually Lawrence was distressed by the sight of Italian workers and soldiers in revolt, his instinctual response to them was another matter. Whereas the aristocrats Aaron meets are not quite human—like the two birdlike gentlemen with whom he spends time—Lawrence humanizes the workers and soldiers whom Aaron and Lilly encounter.

One reason Aaron escaped England in the first place was to be revitalized through the senses. "Italy's best gift to an Englishman," Lawrence wrote, was "a feeling of bravado and almost swaggering carelessness." In Italy, Aaron had crossed the dividing line, and the values of life, though

> ostensibly and verbally the same, were dynamically different. Alas, however, the verbal and the ostensible, the accursed mechanical ideal gains day by day over the spontaneous life-dynamic, so that Italy becomes as idea-bound and as automatic as England: just a business proposition. (*AR*, 178)

But Aaron, like Lawrence, is confused abut where to turn, having rejected class struggle in England. He turns ironically to the one group that is idea-bound—the bourgeois and aristocratic expatriates now living in Italy. They are interesting, even enigmatic to Aaron, but they are also ethereal: they are hardly there for him. They pay his board and listen to his music, but Aaron stays with them mostly out of inertia: he cannot go back to his miners' union nor to his family, nor can he identify with the rebellions taking place in Italy. Lawrence himself must have been genuinely confounded about where to put Aaron:

> Aaron, like everybody else, was rather paralysed by a million sterling, personified in one man [Sir William Franks]. Paralysed, fascinated, overcome. All those three. Only having no final control over his own

106 CLASS, POLITICS, AND THE INDIVIDUAL

make-up he could not drive himself into the money-making or even into the money-having habit. (*AR*, 181)

In a chapter called "Florence," Aaron discusses the regular Saturday concerts at the home of the Marchese and Marchesa Manfredi. Aaron tells his hostess that he can no longer tolerate the music that he associates with parlors or concert halls: music that is harmonious, where the chords and "a number of sounds all sounding together." He agrees with the Marchesa that orechestral music is hateful and adds, "I want to throw bombs" (*AR*, 264). Aaron describes his disdain for the kind of music his wealthy hosts are paying him to play. Although he is aware of his loathing of a culture and a class that he considers stifling, he does not know what to do or where to go. Aaron feels disembodied around his upper-class hosts. When he is convinced to play his flute, Lawrence describes his music "like a bird's singing, in that it had no human emotion or passion or intention or meaning—a ripple and poise of animate sound" (*AR*, 266).

This ethereal quality contrasts sharply with Lawrence's description of workers, around whom Aaron feels more secure. In this passage, Aaron is observing Tuscan farmers in the Piazza della Signoria:

> Their curious full oval cheeks, their tendency to be too fat, to have a belly and heavy limbs. Their close-sitting dark hair. And above all, their sharp, almost acrid, mocking expression, the silent curl of the nose, the eternal challenge, the rock-bottom unbelief, and the subtle fearlessness. The dangerous, subtle, never-dying fearlessness, and the acrid unbelief. But men! Men! A town of men, in spite of everything. The one manly quality, undying, acrid, fearlessness. The eternal challenge of the unquenched human soul. Perhaps too acrid and challenging today, when there is nothing left to challenge. But men—who existed without apology and without justification. Men who would neither justify themselves nor apologize for themselves. Just men. The rarest thing left in our sweet Christendom. (*AR*, 249–50)

The scene echoes that of the third-class passengers, men who Aaron also admired and responded to "at bottom." Feeling himself cut adrift from country and class, Aaron can at least take solace among the company of the working classes in whom an unmistakable fearlessness exists. By contrast, the collection of ex-army officers, knights, barons, and capitalists with whom Aaron spends most of his time appears nostalgic, apologetic, desperate, or un-

Revolution and Retreat   107

happy. As muddled as the political future of England or Italy appears, and as divided as Lawrence was about the need to take political action, the novel leaves little doubt as to which class is in a state of collapse, which, to Aaron, is largely "blowing bubbles." The fundamental tension in *Aaron's Rod* is between the fascination Aaron feels as he listens "spell-bound, watching the bubbles float around his head, hearing them go pop," and his need to find himself in a world that, for Lawrence, was tragically divided by class warfare. Lawrence, like Aaron, was unable to find a long-term satisfactory answer to the question "Where should I be?"

The question is rooted in class awareness. The less Aaron is able to identify with his own class, the more alienated he becomes. When Aaron leaves his work, his union responsibilities and his family, he finalizes his growing estrangement. For most of the book, Aaron rationalizes "that his very being pivoted on the fact of his isolate self-responsibility, aloneness. His intrinsic and central aloneness was the very centre of his being. Break it, and he broke his being" (*AR*, 191). Like Birkin before him and Somers after him, Aaron protests that his "innermost isolation and singleness of his own soul . . . would abide though the skies fell on top of one another, and seven heavens collapsed" (*AR*, 191). But the road away from community leads to alienation, not to liberation, as Aaron discovered:

> He was breaking loose from one connection after another; and what for? Why break every tie? Snap, snap, snap went the bonds and ligatures which bound him to the left that had formed him, the people he had loved or liked. He found all his affections snapping off, all the ties which united him with his own people coming asunder. And why? In God's name, why? What was there instead? There was nothingness. There was just himself, and blank nothingness. (*AR*, 209)

And at the end, faced with the need to answer his own questions, Aaron turns, rather in desperation than in genuine hope, to the kinds of solutions Lilly proposes. On the last page of the novel, Aaron is as openly skeptical of Lilly as the latter seems sure of himself. It is difficult to believe that Lawrence himself was satisfied with what Lilly represents.

Although Lawrence's own peripatetic existence after World War I is consistent with Aaron's stated philosophy of aloneness, Lawrence is not sure how desirable this outlook really is. The future would not be decided by men like Aaron and Lilly. This point is

108   CLASS, POLITICS, AND THE INDIVIDUAL

raised in an unusual aside to the reader. In a letter to Sir William,
Aaron declares a bit desperately that the struggle is everything:

> I don't believe in harmony and people loving one another. I believe in
> the fight and in nothing else. I believe in the fight which is everything.
> And if it is a question of women, I believe in the fight of love, even if it
> blinds me. [. . .] I want the world to hate me, because I can't bear the
> thought that it might love me. For of all things love is the most deadly
> to me, and especially from such a repulsive world as I think this is.
> (*AR*, 308)

Wanting to destroy the old society, Aaron has virtually nothing to
substitute for it; he is unable to act. "Well, here was a letter for a
poor old man to receive," the narrator observes. "But, in the dry-
ness of his withered mind, Aaron got it out of himself. When a
man writes a letter to himself, it is a pity to post it to somebody
else. Perhaps the same is true of a book" (*AR*, 308). The irony of
Aaron's writing to an old baronet about how to fight the system
did not escape Lawrence.

Caught in his own web of inaction and noncommitment, Aaron
ends by repudiating his earlier instincts about workers. After idol-
izing the Tuscan farmers, Aaron is robbed by some Florentine
men. He feels "as if the power of evil had suddenly seized him and
thrown him" (*AR*, 269). The knowledge that he is not safe from a
world he tentatively trusted, maddens him:

> It serves everybody right who rushes enkindled through the street, and
> trusts implicitly in mankind and in the life-spirit, as if mankind and the
> life-spirit were a playground for enkindled individuals. [. . .] Never
> again. Never expose yourself again. Never again absolute trust. It is a
> blasphemy against life, is absolute trust. (*AR*, 270)

"No man is murdered unless he attracts a murderer. Then be not
robbed: it lies within your power" (*AR*, 270), Aaron concludes,
exactly as Birkin before him. Sensibilities like these, especially
when they go unchallenged in the novel, sabotage some of Lawrence's best sensibilities. Aaron's and Lilly's view that workers
could not be trusted with power, that, in fact, no one but people
like themselves should be trusted, a rejection of their initial position against political, sexual, or social intimidation, coercion, or
idealism. As articulated by Lilly these ideals include the following:

> The ideal of life, the ideal that it is better to give than to receive, the
> ideal of liberty, ideal of the brotherhood of man, the ideal of the

Revolution and Retreat   109

sanctity of human life, the ideal of what we call goodness, charity, benevolence, public spiritedness, the ideal of sacrifice for a cause, the ideal of unity and unanimity—all the lot—all the whole beehive of ideals—has all got the modern bee-disease, and gone putrid, stinking. (*AR*, 236)

Any political fight, like the violent street fights between the communists and fascists Aaron often witnesses, is wrong because it kills in the name of these ideals. Lilly's animus is a response to the horror of World War I and the carnage committed in the name of idealism, and the strength of the book lies in the intensity of its attacks against values that prove spurious. Yet by the end of the novel, Aaron and Lilly are doing most of the bullying themselves. Holding stage center, Lilly argues that women should submit to men and that most men should submit "to the heroic soul in a greater man."

For most of Lawrence's iconoclastic heroes, like Aaron and Lilly, breaking every social-personal tie in the absence of alternatives is disintegrative. Having burned his class and social ties, but still desirous of creating new interpersonal norms, Aaron is ready to listen to any idea, however reactionary. Confused by his class identity, feeling dissatisfied with both workers and rulers, Aaron is open to Lilly's theory that the creative power urge—what he calls the "dark, living, fructifying power"—should be utilized for mankind by the greater men. If class and collective struggle are not adequate in dealing with the postwar world, then Lilly's great-man theory of history becomes plausible.

At first eschewing ideology, Lilly becomes trapped by his social ideas. His openly fascist statements at the book's end imply an admission that man is primarily a social creature, even if being social means that the vast majority of mankind submits to a few natural leaders. "Life single, not life double," the "perfect singleness" that he and Aaron so long sought, turns out to be the great ideal and, what is more, a great lie. When all is said and done, what Lilly really finds appealing is, in his words, "a sort of slavery." People, he says, "are not *men;* they are insects and instruments, and their destiny is slavery" (*AR*, 327). Although Lilly admits he has no support, he believes that one day the masses can be won over to this position, "and then they will elect for themselves a proper and healthy and energetic slavery" (*AR*, 327).

This is the same sort of notion put forward in *Kangaroo,* in *Plumed Serpent,* and in *Reflections on the Death of a Porcupine:* the "voluntary acceptance," in Lilly's terms, of "inferior beings to

110 CLASS, POLITICS, AND THE INDIVIDUAL

someone higher . . . a sort of voluntary self-gift of the inferiors" (*AR*, 328). However, Lilly makes clear, once man submits voluntarily, his acceptance "must be held fast by genuine power. Oh yes—no playing and fooling about with it. Permanent and very efficacious power." "You mean military power?" someone asks him. "I do, of course," Lilly answers (*AR*, 328). *Aaron's Rod's* publication in 1922 coincided with the year Mussolini took power, and it was not difficult at the time to take those sentiments at face value.

Like all of Lawrence's novels after *Sons and Lovers*, the end of *Aaron's Rod* represents the start of a new process. Lawrence is not Lilly, despite the author's ambivalent attraction to his protagonist. Lawrence is never for more than a moment committed to Lilly's brand of militarism, and nowhere in his letters or essays does Lawrence ever embrace the fascist cause in Italy, although many fascists of the time found support for their ideas in Lawrence's writings. However much characters like Lilly, Somers, or Kate Leslie might toy with doctrines of voluntary slavery or submission to one's superiors, they themselves are not, finally, ready to submit to anything, let alone to an idealist ideology. Not ready himself to see his beliefs through, Lilly tells Aaron, "I am a vagrant really: or a migrant. I must migrate" (*AR*, 337). Aaron, too, must move on, oscillating, as Lilly puts it, between north and south.

Aaron's Rod is a great statement against the political tragedy of the times. It recoils from the hypocrisies of the war. The work documents the cynicism that the war produced, especially among the soldiers, workers, and artists who were its primary victims. In a number of ways the book is experimental: it is searching for acceptable answers to questions put by consionable men. The novel is self-reflective: on occasion the main character asks, almost of the writer himself: You have stripped me of everything; now what do I have left and for what should I live? *Aaron's Rod* experiments with different, contradictory notions. The idea of the singleness of life is negated by the argument in favor of voluntary slavery, and finally that idea is greatly tempered by Aaron's reluctance to accept it. The powerful presence of class—class distinctions and class differences—is felt throughout the novel. Lawrence presents a fairly accurate picture of the class struggles in Italy in the early 1920s. Yet, in the end, Lawrence is unwilling to commit his characters to the social and political fight that surrounds them. So the novel's portrayal of Aaron and Lilly creates other Ishmaels and, with nothing for them to go back or forward to—neither country, family, nor class—more social orphans.

Revolution and Retreat 111

Kangaroo: In the Midst of Battle

In 1922, the Lawrences went to Australia. In a five-week period beginning in June, Lawrence wrote *Kangaroo,* the first novel he wrote outside Europe. He left the continent, Lawrence explained in his autobiographical novel, because "he had made up his mind that everything was done for, played out, finished, and he must go to a new country" (*K,* 8). Assuming the persona of Richard Lovat Somers, Lawrence explained his withdrawal to the "do-as-you-please liberty" of Australia: he did not mean to escape politics altogether, as this novel and his next one, *Plumed Serpent,* made clear. "I feel," Somers says to his wife Harriet:

> I *must* fight out something with mankind yet. I haven't finished with my fellow men. I've got a struggle with them yet. I intend to move with men and get men to move with me before I die. [. . .] I've got to struggle with men and the world of men for a time yet. (*K,* 64)

Somers's struggle with men and the world of men and his desire to change society are just two of the concerns apparent in *Aaron's Rod:* the wish of the individual to grow and create—in Somers's case to write—through one's own selfhood; the need for aloneness; and betrayal, such as what Aaron felt when he yielded in any way to the masses, or to political, fixed idealisms. But *Kangaroo* is not merely an extension of *Aaron's Rod:* it adds a number of dimensions to Lawrence's lifelong ambivalent relationship to men, to society, and to political struggle.

For one, *Kangaroo* is clearly coming to grips with Lawrence's ideas about democracy, fascism, the social role of art, and the role of the individual caught between the decline of postwar Europe and the rise of the militant left- and right-wing politics. *Kangaroo* is reflective of a number of essays Lawrence wrote about these subjects during the early 1920s: "Democracy," published within a year of the novel; "Introduction to *Memoirs of the Foreign Legion,*" written about January 1922; and "Surgery for the Novel—Or a Bomb," written about February 1923. Of these essays, "Democracy" articulates the major ideas then dominating Lawrence's social and political thinking, ideas that were in their incipient form in *Aaron's Rod.* These are notions that Somers grapples with during his encounters with Jack Callcott, the novel's so-called "average," democratic man; with Benjamin Cooley— "Kangaroo" of the novel—the leader of an anticapitalist, antisocialist, semifascist movement of Australian Diggers; and

112   Class, Politics, and the Individual

with Willie Struthers, a socialist labor leader. A large portion of the novel is devoted to testing these arguments about democracy. Not until the end of the novel does Somers reject all political ideologies and leave Australia for the relative calm of North America.

"Democracy" is Lawrence's most comprehensive statement about what he considered the destructive idealism of his age: political theorizing based on the principles of the equality of man, Christian love, socialist brotherhood, or the need for the redistribution of property. Lawrence felt increasingly hostile to all these concepts, most of which he witnessed in Italy. In his essay, the author expressed his growing belief that "the State is a dead ideal. *Nation* is a dead ideal. Democracy and Socialism are dead ideals. They are one and all just *contrivances* for the supplying of the lowest material needs of a people" (*Ph 1*, 702). Political theory was a "trick of the devil" (*Ph 1*, 705). Politics, idealism, property, and materialism all formed "a fixed, static entity, an abstraction, an extraction from the living body of life" (*Ph 1*, 711). Lawrence identified such abstractions with Whitman's "one Identity, the *En-Masse*," that "horrible nullification of true identity and being" (*Ph 1*, 709). Politics, Lawrence wrote in this essay, was "just another, extra-large, commercial wrangle over buying and selling—nothing else. . . . *Politics ideal! Political Idealists!* What rank gewgaw and nonsense!" (*Ph 1*, 703).

Against these ghouls of idealism, Lawrence posed an ideal of his own—a new man, one who was not so mechanical, materialistic, or, overall, so utilitarian. His hero was called "the actual living, creative quick," the "spontaneous and single" individual, "the living self," or the "spontaneous, single, pure being." Modern man had two choices: "There are the two great temptations of the fall of man, the fall from spontaneous, single, pure being, into what we call materialism or automatism or mechanism of the self." Either we are to "preserve the soul free and spontaneous," or be "degraded into a fixed activity, there must be *no fixed direction*. There can be no ideal goal for human life. Any ideal goal means mechanization, materialism, and nullity" (*Ph 1*, 715). Sentiments like these explain why Somers ultimately rejects both Cooley's and Struthers's politics.

The problem of democracy as Lawrence experienced it, first in Australia and then in North America, was that the great illusion of equality and oneness reduced men to "automatic units, determined by mechanical law." This reduction was "horribly true of modern democracy—socialism, conservatism, bolshevism, liberalism, re-

Revolution and Retreat

publicanism, communism: all alike" (*Ph 1*, 717). Somers is temporarily attracted to Ben Cooley's fascist movement because it is based on what Somers calls "the mystery of lordship" and not on the equality of men. For a time after the war, when Lawrence held democracy accountable for the reduction and the bullying of humanity, he toyed with this notion of "lordship," which he defines in *Kangaroo* as follows:

> The mystery of innate, natural, sacred priority. The other mystic relationship between men, which democracy and equality try to deny and obliterate. Not any arbitrary caste or birth aristocracy. But the mystic recognition of difference and innate priority, the joy of obedience and the sacred responsibility of authority. (*K*, 105)

Inevitably Somers, like Lawrence, came to reject this notion since the character hated to submit to any leadership himself.

In addition to ridiculing the false idea of brotherhood and Christian love, Kangaroo's movement appeals to Somers because it is not concerned with the equal distribution of property, "the one principle," Lawrence wrote in "Democracy," "that governs all the *isms*. [. . .] All ideas work down to the sheer materialism which is their intrinsic reality, at last. It doesn't matter, now, who has the property. They have all lost their being over it" (*Ph 1*, 717). The mystical language used by Kangaroo obviated the materialist trap of all political ideologies. True to the essay, *Kangaroo* is expressive of the alternative Lawrence puts forward: the spontaneous man, unimpressed with programs concerning property and the supposed equality of man, listening to the god in his soul, can replace the political materialist who wants to subject mankind to one or another set of largely economic constraints. The final paragraph of "Democracy" sets the tone of the challenges Somers faces:

> Every attempt at preordaining a new material world only adds another straw to the load that already has broken so many backs. If we are to keep our backs unbroken, we must deposit all property on the ground, and learn to walk without it. We must stand aside. And when many men stand aside, they stand in a new world; a new world of man has come to pass. This is the Democracy, the new order. (*Ph 1*, 718)

Somers finds that going to Australia with many of these thoughts in mind but encountering a democracy with very real needs concerning property and its distribution are antithetical. Within the materialist, class-structured context of Australia, Somers discovers

114 CLASS, POLITICS, AND THE INDIVIDUAL

that it is next to impossible to implement his own idealist ideas about spontaneity, instinct, and a creative, rather than preordained response to the material world. *Kangaroo* is a complex and rewarding book for this reason: it acknowledges that a real world of class, property, and revolution exists, while it simultaneously probes that world to see if it is pervious to a new order based on a different set of assumptions.

The novel is reflective of two other essays Lawrence wrote in 1922, the year this work was finished. "Introduction to *Memoirs of the Foreign Legion*" explains to what extent the war still burned in Lawrence's consciousness and why the chapter called "Nightmare" is by far the longest section in the novel. For humanity to advance, Lawrence argued in his essay, every man had to come to terms with the war and the violence, hatred, and corruption it unleashed:

> There is no gainsaying it. We all fell. Let us not try to wriggle out of it. We fell into hideous depravity of hating the human soul; a purulent smallpox of the spirit we had. It was shameful, shameful, shameful, in every country and in all of us. [. . .] A purulent smallpox of the vicious spirit, vicious against the deep soul that pulses in the blood. (*Ph 2*, 358)

To cleanse the soul, "full of the running sores of the war," it was necessary to face the reality of it squarely, "with bitter and wincing realization. We have to take the disease into our consciousness and let it go through our soul, like some virus. We have got to realize and then we can surpass" (*Ph 2*, 358). To a large degree, *Aaron's Rod* and *Kangaroo* try to achieve a purgation of the war. Cooley's and Struthers's militance is largely a reaction to the war. Fundamentally, Somers rejects both men for the same reason he hated the fighting: they both represent political coercion. However much Somers and Lawrence want to see social change, they fear a class war in which men must submit—as they must in any battle. Lawrence's conclusion to *"Memoirs"* prepares the reader for the ending of *Kangaroo*, when Somers turns his back on the two radicals:

> All modern militarism is foul. It shall go. A man I am, and above machines, and it shall go, forever, because I have found it vile, vile, too vile ever to experience again. Cannons shall go. Never again shall trenches be dug. They *shall* not, for I am a man, and such things are within the power of man, to break and make. I have said it, and as long as blood beats in my veins, I mean it. (*Ph 2*, 359)

Somers comes to understand that his social stand-offishness will avail nothing: individuality is a losing proposition. But worst of all

Revolution and Retreat   115

is the wholesale coercion that a social revolution entails. After experimenting with this notion in *Plumed Serpent*—that to advance society one had to grab it by the scruff of the neck—Lawrence virtually abandoned politics. *Lady Chatterley's Lover*—originally entitled *Tenderness*—was the author's reaction to the social bullying pictured in *Kangaroo* and in *Plumed Serpent*.

"Surgery for the Novel—Or a Bomb," finished in early 1923, spells out Lawrence's growing conviction that fiction and the portrayal of social change cannot be separated without doing injury to the novel. Somers is courted by Kangaroo and Struthers precisely because he is a successful writer, and both men understand how literature can effect social change. The future of the novel, Lawrence wrote in the essay, includes breaking "a way through, like a hole in the wall." *Kangaroo* is partially the story of how to integrate art and politics. Somers continually tests his craft by the social struggles around him. By the 1920s, Lawrence was convinced that a great deal of literature was wasted by its profound subjectivity, its concern with self rather than with the greater reality of the world. In "Surgery for the Novel," Lawrence took Joyce to task for the latter's subjectivity:

> It's awful. And it's childish. It really is childish, after a certain age, to be absorbedly self-conscious. One has to be self-conscious at seventeen: still a little self-conscious at twenty-seven; but if we are going it strong at thirty-seven, then it is a sign of arrested development, nothing else. And if it is still continuing at forty-seven, it is obviously senile precocity. (*Ph 1*, 518)

The future of the novel, he continued, must include a vision "for a new state of things, when this democratic-industrial-lovey-dovey-darling-take-me-to-mamma state of things is bust" (*Ph 1*, 520). *Kangaroo* and *Plumed Serpent* are attempts to break through the democratic industrial "wall." At first, Lawrence warned, the public will be horrified to "see a new glaring hole in what was [its] cosy wall." The responsibility of art, however, is to prepare the public for the changes to come. Then "gradually, first one and then another of the sheep filters through the gap, and finds a new world outside."

Kangaroo begins with echoes of the bitter lessons Aaron had come to learn: the self in sheer isolation, going nowhere, advances neither itself nor one's fellow men. Clearly Lawrence was determined to move away from the pervasive gloom and frustration of *Aaron's Rod*. Although World War I still haunts the main charac-

116 CLASS, POLITICS, AND THE INDIVIDUAL

ters, Somers and Harriet, talk about the war is limited to the important "Nightmare" chapter. Tired of the chatter of Lilly's sort about the "innermost, integral, unique self," which will nonetheless submit voluntarily to an even greater self, Somers insists that he "move with men and get men to move with me." To do this successfully, he must maintain at least minimum ties with the "average men" of Australia, a country Somers calls "absolutely and flatly democratic, *a terre* democratic. Demos was here his own master, undisputed, and therefore quite calm about it" (*K,* 16–17). The usual ambivalence of Lawrence's characters in regard to their social class surfaces here, with Somers feeling smothered by the common man and by the leveling effect of democracy. Somers's love-hate relationship with Australia, its people, and its socialist and fascist movements, is captured in his relationship to Jack Callcott, a worker who is Kangaroo's lieutenant. Their friendship brings out all the contradictions inherent in Lawrence's view of class. Like Somers, Lawrence wanted to participate in the activities of workers, but he continually shied away from such commitments. A deep and widening gap was created between Lawrence's search for an inner "Dark God" of instinct and spontaneity and his acknowledgment of material circumstances. When Lawrence describes both Somers's friendship with and then growing fear of Callcott, the schism between Lawrence's social perspective and his psychic one becomes more apparent. In *Kangaroo,* most of the major thematic conflicts develop as a result of how Somers perceives events. A social event is frequently translated into an aesthetic or psychological one. Often the extreme shifts in Somers's feelings about this or that struggle or character are explained by Lawrence's indecision as to what should take precedence: man as a creature of class and society, or man as a creature of instincts and feelings.

When Somers meets Jack Callcott, an immediate physical rapport develops since, like Jack, "Somers was of the people himself, and he had that alert *instinct* of the common people, the instinctive knowledge of what his neighbor was wanting and thinking, and the instinctive necessity to answer" (*K,* 31). Lawrence thereby makes an immediate distinction between classes, one not based on social or economic exigencies but on how members of each class react to one another, in ways that are inscrutable to the upper classes:

> With the other classes, there is a certain breach between individual and individual, and not much goes across except what is intended to go

Revolution and Retreat

across. But with the common people, and with most Australians, there is no breach. The communication is silent and involuntary, the give and take flows like waves from person to person, and each one knows: unless he is foiled by speech. (*K*, 31)

The upper classes are less intuitive. They have

> a set preference for the non-intuitive forms of communication, for deliberate speech. What is not said is supposed not to exist: that is almost a code of honour with the other classes. With the true common people, only that which is *not* said is of any vital significance. (*K*, 32)

This intuitive response keeps alive, for a while, Somers's interest in Jack and the Digger movement and then in Struthers's trade unionism. If he could not join with workers on a social, political, or economic basis, an instinctive communication kept Lawrence's connection with his class from withering completely: "Much as he [Somers] wanted to be alone, to stand clear from the weary business of unanimity with everybody, he had never chosen really to suspend this power of intuitive response" (*K*, 32). Just as Lilly was chided for absurdly declaring his isolation, all the while being dependent on others, Somers is parodied, by his wife and by the narrator, for his mercurial intuitive responses. With no real ideological basis for his lightning-quick, gut reactions, Somers is an elusive character: "Perhaps it was difficult to locate any definite Somers," the narrator writes, "any one individual in all this ripple of animation and communication. The man himself seemed lost in the bright aura of his rapid consciousness" (*K*, 33). This quality accounts for people's fascination with him; it is also responsible for his ephemeral commitment to Jack, to Cooley, or to Struthers, in fact, to any cause whatsoever.

Lawrence identifies with Somers but is quick to point out his protagonist's vulnerability as he simultaneously poses two contrary frames of reference: the social with the subject—what Lawrence calls Somers's "bright quickness" and "brightly-burning bush of consciousness." Harriet, continually articulating the author's self-doubts, ridicules the untenable positions her husband takes as he straddles these two worlds. The more Somers takes an active interest in Kangaroo's Digger movement, the more Harriet undermines and ridicules him. She, at least, knows that he is just experimenting with ideas with which he is basically uncomfortable. The breach between Somers's aesthetic response to the world and the social commitments that are needed to "move with men and get men to move" is far too great for her husband to bridge.

118   CLASS, POLITICS, AND THE INDIVIDUAL

Early in the novel, for example, when Somers begins toying with Cooley's peculiar brand of fascism, Jack tells him, "We're not having the women in, if we can help it. Don't believe in it, do you?" Somers answers, "Not in real politics, I don't" (*K*, 92). Harriet is a foil to Somers's social idealism, which now has become perverted, rather like Lilly's toward the end of *Aaron's Rod*, where he preached a doctrine similar to Jack's. Harriet sees the irony of Jack's position. In this case, both the authorial voice and Harriet's are the same: "In short, he was to be the lord and master, and she the humble slave. [. . .] She was to submit to the mystic man and male in him, with reverence, and even a little awe, like a woman before the altar of the great Hermes" (*K*, 176). It is not bossing she necessarily objects to, but that one such as her husband should have these pretensions:

> How could she believe in such a man! If he had been naturally a master of men, general of an army, or manager of some great steel works, with thousands of men under him—then, yes, she could have acknowledged the *master* part of the bargain, if not the lord. Whereas, as it was, he was the most forlorn and isolated creature in the world, without even a dog to his command. He was so isolated he was hardly a man at all, among men. He had absolutely nothing but her. (*K*, 177)

The same, of course, can be said of Lilly and Aaron, men who had flashes of social aspirations that gradually became dominated by private considerations and notions of elitism.

Increasingly, Somers is held captive by his "brightly-burning bush of consciousness." He cannot, nor can any character, sustain the language of politics or class. Although a material basis for revolution certainly existed in Italy and Australia, social issues are replaced by aesthetic ones in *Kangaroo*, as Lawrence begins to reject the social and political categories he originally set up. When Somers meets Kangaroo, he reacts to him as if Cooley were an object of art:

> Kangaroo sat there with the rapt look on his face: a pondering, eternal look, like the eternity of the lamb of God grown into a sheep. So the man sat there, with his wide-eyed, rapt face sunk forward to his breast, very beautiful, and as eternal as if it were a dream: so absolute. A wonderful thing for a sculptor. For Kangaroo was really ugly. [. . .] And yet even his body had become beautiful, to Somers—one might love it intensely, every one of its contours, its roundness and down-ward-drooping heaviness. (*K*, 112)

Revolution and Retreat 119

"Why, the man is like a god, I love him," Somers says to his awestruck, "astonished self." Somers is in a rapture that holds him enthralled until his fascination turns into its opposite. The result of his emotional ephemera is that he is later disgusted by the ideals to which he is initially attracted. Later on, when Kangaroo demands more of Somers than he is prepared to give, Somers's love for Kangaroo turns into hatred. Identifying with no social cause, Somers discards Kangaroo's will-to-love as an abstraction and as a threat to his own "mere manliness." Kangaroo tries to bully Somers into submitting his individualism and his elitism to a new social order, something the latter cannot do. Now the godlike Kangaroo becomes a monster sent from hell:

> He had become again hideous, with a long yellowish face and black eyes close together, and a cold mindless, dangerous hulk of his shoulders. For a moment Somers was afraid of him, as of some great ugly idol that might strike. He felt the intense hatred of the man coming at him in cold waves. He stood up in a kind of horror in front of the great, close-eyed, horrible thing that was not Kangaroo. Yes, a thing, not a whole man. A great Thing, a horror. (*K*, 214)

When Somers reacts to Struthers—Lawrence's caricatured notion of a working-class leader—he does not respond to Struthers's politics or even to his xenophobic attitude toward non-Australian labor. Somers finds Struthers physically repulsive. "He's shrewd," Somers tells Kangaroo. "Only I don't like him physically— something thin and hairy and spiderish. I don't want to touch him. But he's a force, he's *something*" (*K*, 209). Once more, ideological considerations give way to aesthetic ones.

Kangaroo outlines his program for Australia, a program that is based on Lilly's proposition that most men crave a leader who will lead them to what Cooley calls the "voice of life," a leader who will "shelter mankind from the madness and the evil of anti-life." It is a program for which Lawrence himself had a great deal of sympathy as the essay "Death of a Porcupine" and, later, *Plumed Serpent* show. Cooley's argument reads like Lawrence's version of Dostoyevsky's "The Grand Inquisitor":

> Life is cruel—and above all things man needs to be reassured and suggested into his new issues. And he needs to be relieved from this terrible responsibility of governing himself when he doesn't know what he wants, and has no aim towards which to govern himself. Man again needs a father. [. . .] Man needs a quiet gentle father who uses his

120 CLASS, POLITICS, AND THE INDIVIDUAL

authority in the name of living life, and who is absolutely stern against anti-life. (*K*, 110–11)

Because he is attracted to this type of benign dictatorship himself, Lawrence articulated no real criticism of it. Instead, he has Somers react intuitively to the person of Kangaroo: "The man had a beautiful voice, when he was really talking. It was like a flute, a wood instrument. And his face [. . .] took on an extraordinary beauty of its own, a glow as if it were suffused with light. And the eyes shone with a queer, holy light" (*K*, 111). When Kangaroo explains why man needs to be benignly enslaved, Somers sees his face as "very beautiful, and as eternal as if it were a dream: so absolute."

Somers's physical reactions to Kangaroo and later to Struthers often veil Lawrence's ideological responses to these two men. The ideological *isms*, Lawrence said over and over again in his essays and in his history text, are irrelevant, misleading, and destructive. "No sort of politics will help the country," Somers tells Jaz, Callcott's friend. Somers now speaks rather openly for Lawrence:

I don't really care about politics. Politics is no more than your country's housekeeping. If I had to swallow my whole life up in housekeeping, I wouldn't keep house at all; I'd sleep under a hedge. Same with a country and politics and social stuff. I'd rather have the moon for a motherland. (*K*, 59)

"Politics are a game for the base people with no human soul in them," Somers tells Harriet (*K*, 97).

The correct response to a Kangaroo or Struthers, according to Somers, is to reject politics altogether, to embrace instead a new religious idea based on "living and not having." Somers visualizes a born-again Christianity that "grew up for centuries without having anything at all to do with politics—just a *feeling*, a belief" (*K*, 96). Revolutions, he says, are "out of date." This dichotomy between feeling and politics runs throughout the book. For example when William James (Jaz) refers to his leader Cooley, he tells Somers, "It's wonderful what a spell he can cast over you" (*K*, 128). And since Somers and Jaz come from a working-class background, Somers imagines that they share a physical connection that goes beyond rational thought: "It was a strange, different bond of sympathy united them from that that subsisted between Somers and Jack, or Somers and Kangaroo. Hardly sympathy at all, but an ancient sort of root knowledge" (*K*, 129). Lawrence describes Call-

Revolution and Retreat 121

cott's eye as "secretive"; the word "soul" comes to replace "mind," and Somers begins to talk about the "life-mystery" as a replacement for political involvement.

The way Somers reacts to the world, spontaneously, physically, with deep feeling, is reminiscent of the way Paul Morel, Ursula, and Birkin responded to the world. The difference, however, is that Somers is caught in a web of politics and struggle where subjective responses are not adequate. As much as Lawrence turned to the language of mysticism—"root knowledge" as a stronger force than, say, class struggle—he signaled that he was not satisfied with this sort of escapism. After all, Somers had come to Australia looking for new social fields to plow. He was tired of writing essays and poems in Europe, a continent where "everything was done for, played out, finished." So Lawrence kept Somers's limitations, limitations imposed by his quicksilver and egotistical responses to the world:

> He didn't hate anybody in particular, nor even any class or body of men. He loathed politicians, and the well-bred darling young men of the well-to-do middle classes made his bile stir. But he didn't fret himself about them specially. The off-hand self-assertive working people of Australia made him feel diabolic on their score sometimes. But as a rule the particulars were not in evidence, all the rocks were submerged, and his bile just swirled diabolically for no particular reason at all. He just felt generally diabolical, and tried merely to keep enough good sense not to turn his temper in any particular direction. (*K*, 164)

Harriet taunts Somers: "You think that nothing but goodness and virtue and wonderfulness comes out of you. You don't know how small and mean and ugly you are to other people" (*K*, 164).

Lawrence, therefore, cannot be confused with Somers. The author is pulled in the direction of Cooley and Struthers because they at least have concrete programs for society. He resembles Sommers up to a point because Lawrence questioned any program based on what he called the rigidities and abstractions of all idealisms, particularly political ones. But he sensed the inadequacies of his hero's position, and the following narrative observation is certainly applicable to Somers:

> The greatest hero that ever existed was heroic only whilst he kept the throbbing inner union with something, God, or Fatherland, or woman. [. . .] A man must strive onward, but from the root of marriage, marriage with God, with wife, with mankind. Like a tree that is

122   CLASS, POLITICS, AND THE INDIVIDUAL

rooted, always growing and flowering away from its root, so is a vitally active man. (*K*, 165)

Clearly the contradiction for Somers, as it was for Lawrence, was the desire to be within a stream of human activity and still function as Lawrence forever said he wanted to: "The man by himself," in Somers's words. "Each man to himself! Each man back to his own soul! Alone, alone, with his own soul alone" (*K*, 287). Most of the time, unable to resolve this antithesis, Somers swings between extremes, from veneration for the godlike Kangaroo, feeling a "root knowledge" with fellow workers, to expressing sentiments like the following, reminiscent of the worst moments of Birkin, Lilly, or Aaron: "Damn the man in the street. Damn the collective soul, it's a dead rat in a hole. Let humanity scratch its own lice" (*K*, 287).

The dilemma posed by *Kangaroo* is one that Lawrence cannot resolve—except by flight. "This place is no good," again becomes a refrain as it did in *Lost Girl, Women in Love,* and *Aaron's Rod.* Somers used his instincts, his intuitive knowledge, to act as a foil to Cooley's and Struthers's political theorizing. Now such immediate physical responses become a rationale for leaving Australia. Just as he eventually came to loathe the sight of Kangaroo, Somers comes gradually to believe that Australia itself has betrayed him. Now, instead of allowing his natural spontaneity to at least come to grips with Cooley's or Struthers's world, Somers is all but ready to make the world itself disappear. In *Sons and Lovers, Rainbow,* and *Women in Love,* nature was often a substitute for the social world. The abstractions characters found in political or social idealisms were offset by the intense physical contacts they found in the world of nature. But as Somers feels increasingly pressured to truly participate in the activities of men, he begins to blame not only himself, but the dead-endedness of the physical world for his inability to move.

In *Sons and Lovers* and in *Rainbow,* nature had a certain life of its own. Fairly independent of the narrator's frame of mind, it was a reliable place in which to escape. In *Kangaroo,* however, physical nature eventually becomes a reflection of Somers's increasing despair and subjectivity. "As was always the case," the narrator says of Somers, "the land and the world disappeared as night fell, as if the day had been an illusion, and the sky came bending down" (*K*, 137). The old world—the world of war, revolution, and political idealism—is a world to be blanked out. One should "be in a new

Revolution and Retreat   123

way denizen of a new plane, walking by oneself. There would be a real new way to take. And the mechanical earth quite obliterated, sunk out" (*K*, 137). As Somers becomes more and more disenchanted with politics and the self-serving idealism of Kangaroo and Struthers, he turns to nature. But Somers finds that he has been let down there, too. The Australian countryside is "curiously unapproachable to him." As Somers ends up in full retreat from his wife, neighbors, and newly formed social ties, this disintegrative process extends to nature, and the countryside comes to reflect Somers's state of mind. Australia no longer has a life to offer; it is "without a core. There was no heart in it all, it seemed hollow" (*K*, 311). Australia is covered by "a vast endless, sun-hot, afternoon sleep with the world a mirage" (*K*, 314). Somers gets ready to sail to America. When he and Harriet depart, it is with a great measure of sorrow that their personal and social efforts have failed: "Sydney, and the war harbour. They crossed over once more in the blue afternoon. Kangaroo dead. Sydney lying on its many-lobed blue harbour, in the blue air. Revolution—nothingness. Nothing could ever matter" (*K*, 364–65).

Kangaroo is perhaps one of the sharpest and most painfully developed accounts of the dilemmas Lawrence faced in the years between the publication of *Women in Love* and *Plumed Serpent*—books in which war and revolution are set in contrast to the leading characters' psychic concerns. When, at the end of these novels, the major characters move on, it is at an enormous psychological cost. They are, at least for the moment, caught in a no-man's land—suspended between private and public concerns.

The Plumed Serpent: The Politics of Religion

In *Kangaroo*, Somers was speaking for Lawrence when he argued that life should not begin with a form—and by a form he primarily meant a rigid political outlook—but with a new feeling. "A new religious idea must gradually spring up and ripen before there could be any constructive change," the narrator of *Kangaroo* had said. "Then men with soul and with passionate truth in them must control the world's material riches and supplies: absolutely put possessions out of the reach of the mass of mankind, and let life begin to live again, in place of this struggle for existence, or struggle for wealth" (*K*, 97). This new religious idea could come from neither Cooley nor Struthers; for the former had become

124 CLASS, POLITICS, AND THE INDIVIDUAL

obsessed with "one central principle in the world: the principle of life" and the latter believed in the idealism of "the rule of the People." After quitting Europe, with its destructive ideological obsessions, Somers was "tired of one central principle in the world." He wanted, as apparently Lawrence did, to stand before a sensibility, to maintain a mystery about man, to keep man from being subjected to analysis and dissection. "Let's get off it," Somers told Kangaroo. "I like to know the gods beyond me. Let's start as men with the great gods beyond us" (*K*, 214).

Somers felt caught between the leveling effects of democracy and socialism and Kangaroo's "benign" fascism. Hoping for social change, dissatisfied with his perpetual isolation from other men, Somers was equally fearful of becoming submerged in political struggle and the discipline such struggle requires. At the end, unable to resolve this contradiction, Somers defended his own "mere manliness" and his all-too-vulnerable "living spirit." When he left for America, he was not entirely without hope. Before his departure, he assured Jaz that "I won't give up the flag of our real civilised consciousness. I'll give up the ideals. But not the aware, self-responsible, deep consciousness that we've gained. I won't go back on that, Jaz, though Kangaroo did say I was the enemy of civilisation" (*K*, 356). He told his friend that indeed he was "the enemy of this machine civilisation and this ideal civilisation" but that he would continue to fight for

> the deep, self-responsible consciousness in man, which is what I mean by civilisation. In that sense of civilisation, I'd fight forever for the flag, and try to carry it on into deeper, darker places. It's an adventure, Jaz, like any other. And when you realise what you're doing, it's perhaps the best adventure. (*K*, 356)

The Plumed Serpent, published in 1925, is just such an adventure.

None of his other works more sharply focuses the dichotomies that troubled Lawrence: religion and politics, flesh and spirit, the desire to be part of mankind and the need to be free of all social contact. *The Plumed Serpent* is simultaneously the most political and the most religious and mystical of all his novels. It represents Lawrence's attempt to write a novel that contained a fairly doctrinaire religious-political program, something he warned against in his 1925 essay, "The Novel." There he wrote that the novel "is the highest form of human expression" because "it is so incapable of the absolute. [. . .] There may be didactic bits, but they aren't

Revolution and Retreat

the novel" (*Ph 2*, 416). Too much purpose, too much of the novelist with an idea of himself and how life should be, Lawrence wrote, is what ails the modern novel:

> The Modern novelist is possessed, hag-ridden, by such a stale old "purpose," or idea-of-himself, that his inspiration succumbs. Of course he denies having any didactic purpose at all: because a purpose is supposed to be like catarrh, something to be ashamed of. But he's got it. They've all got it: the same sniveling purpose. (*Ph 2*, 418)

At the same time, he believed that all art was "utterly dependent on" a philosophy:

> The metaphysic or philosophy may not be anywhere very accurately stated and may be quite unconscious, in the artist, yet it is a metaphysic that governs men at the time, and is by all men more or less comprehended, and lived. Men live and see according to some gradually developing and gradually withering vision. This vision exists also as a dynamic idea or metaphysic—exists first as such. Then it is unfolded into life and art. Our vision, our belief, our metaphysic is wearing woefully thin, and the art is wearing absolutely threadbare. We have no future; neither for our hopes nor our aims nor our art. It has all gone gray and opaque. (*PF,* 57)

The Plumed Serpent attempts to juggle all these considerations, which is why this novel is so difficult. The work contains both a vision and a repudiation of this vision. In the novel, Lawrence wrestles with himself over every issue—religious, sexual, and political—exploring the possibilities of social, political, and personal change. The plumed serpent is itself a mixed metaphor. Quetzacoatl—half bird, half snake—suggests a struggle and a unity of opposites.

Lawrence set out to do in *Plumed Serpent* what he failed to achieve in *Kangaroo:* create a language that would lend itself to a new spiritual and social order more readily than the political ideologies of Cooley or Struthers. He chose the language of myth and evoked ancient Mexican gods, various symbols involving nature, and the rituals of dance and music. Whereas Cooley and Struthers were forever articulating and explaining their programs, Lawrence, now proposed another sort of understanding, one aimed more at the emotions than at the intellect. Myth, Lawrence hoped, with its attendant symbols drawn from nature, would reach down into the human psyche, into the blood, without the

126   CLASS, POLITICS, AND THE INDIVIDUAL

need for mental description. In this way the gap between the classes might be bridged, and class struggle made unnecessary. One of the assumptions of *Plumed Serpent* is expressed early in the book by Kate: "All the liberty, all the progress, all the socialism in the world would not help him [the Mexican Indian]. Nay, it would only help further to destroy him" (*PS*, 54). In *Plumed Serpent*, Lawrence wanted to achieve what he was unable to do in his previous novels: a community of all the people, not one based on class, politics, or property relations. Myth became a vehicle for saying that all men share a prepolitical heritage, one that goes beyond class. Myth supplied the dark, deep gods before which all men could stand. Myth would be, as the narrator in *Kangaroo* put it, "an answer to the strange creative urge, the God-whisper, which is the one and only everlasting motive for everything" (*K*, 301). In *Plumed Serpent*, men share the same blood consciousness. The ancient Mexican-Indian gods are supposed to simultaneously unite men and still allow for the privacy of the individual, a synthesis that had always eluded Lawrence's characters.

The serpent and the bird—Quetzalcoatl—gather to themselves not only all the dualisms Lawrence wanted to synthesize but also all the contradictions this new religion itself posed. Both components of the Mexican god were equally genuine to Lawrence. The symbol explicitly acknowledged the complexities of life, that one could not—as Kangaroo or Struthers had tried to do—limit the individual by recognizing only his material or his spiritual well-being. The plumed serpent, as metaphor, declared that life was a composite of contraries. The god existed "to merge again into the deep bath of life," to bring together life's contradictions. The god was a mixture of earth and sky, body and spirit, materialism and spiritualism, instincts and the intellect: "All a confusion of contradictory gleams of meaning, Quetzalcoatl. But why not?" (*PS*, 61)" Kate Leslie, the central character in this book, and for the most part, Lawrence's spokesman, is described as "weary to death of definite meanings, and a God of one fixed purport. Gods should be iridescent, like the rainbow in the storm. Man creates a God in his own image, and the gods grow old along with the men that made them" (*PS*, 61). The language and themes of *Plumed Serpent* depend on Lawrence's unresolved beliefs; namely, that class does and does not make the man or his society. This in large measure explains why he chose a language with religious and mystical symbols, why the language is deliberately ambiguous. It was meant to suggest a myriad of possibilities—as Lawrence felt life did. The

Revolution and Retreat

mythic quality of *Plumed Serpent* served also to reconcile forces, synthesize those universal elements with which Lawrence always seemed to be wrestling. Of these symbols, that of the plumed serpent is key.

The Plumed Serpent begins with very much the same political recognitions and personal disappointments that characterize *Aaron's Rod* and *Kangaroo*. These three postwar novels are set against a backdrop of class turmoil, revolution, and war, and a group of intellectuals and artists—Lilly, Aaron, Somers, and Kate—who are cut loose from any of the conventional moorings. Kate leaves her country, Ireland, for many of the same reasons as Aaron, Lilly, and Somers left theirs:

> In England, in Ireland, during the war and the revolution, she had known *spiritual* fear. The ghastly fear of the rabble; and during the war, nations were nearly all rabble. The terror of the rabble that, mongrel-like, wanted to break the free *spirit* in individual men and women. It was the cold, collective lust of millions of people, to break the spirit in the outstanding individuals. They wanted to break this spirit. [. . .] The rabble. (*PS*, 148–49)

Curiously, however, Aaron and Lilly chose to retreat to Italy, Somers to Australia, and Kate to Mexico, countries that hummed with the collective energies of people on the move—the rabble. Like Lawrence, despite Kate's fears of being dragged down by the "uncreated masses"—the Mexican Indians—she is drawn to men who are making history. She shares with "outstanding individuals" like Aaron, Lilly, and Somers the same ambivalences: the fear of being dragged down by the mob, and the fear of being left behind by the social revolution.

Lawrence started each of these novels with the historical fact of social upheaval. He rather convincingly showed that a social basis existed for the revolutionary society Mexico had become, that class antagonisms partially explain why the Mexicans were killing their landowners and repudiating the Catholic church. He rejected taking an overt class position, but the presence of class in these three novels is inescapable. Most often Lawrence is of two minds about what course to set for the social ship, or whether, in fact, the elite need to be on that ship at all. This confusion is largely an effect of his simultaneous avowal and disavowal of a class outlook. For example, Lawrence pictures a Mexico controlled by a land-owning class, a corrupt government and its accomplice, the church; next he denies that a Mexican revolution should be the result of class inter-

128   CLASS, POLITICS, AND THE INDIVIDUAL

ests. After detailing the nature of class struggle in Mexico, Lawrence argued that this mass movement was inherently self-destructive, and that nothing positive could come of it. The novel begins by portraying social alliances in Mexico rather accurately and ends by turning toward mysticism and religion. That Lawrence was genuinely unsure of where he stood is indicated by the competing thematic approaches of this novel, one of which is sociological, the other, based on myth and the nonrational forces of man and the universe. Perhaps the most pointed way these dualisms get expressed in *The Plumed Serpent* is through Lawrence's portrayal of the Indians: they personify the most negative, atavistic qualities of mankind and, at the same time, humanity's most potentially redemptive features.

Although the novel attaches much importance to the Mexican Indians, Lawrence is uncertain about their social and historical role. Cipriano tells his men, "Our gods hate a kneeling man." The time has come for the Indian to take his civilization into his own hands—away from the North Americans. At the same time, Lawrence is frightened at the thought of these "half-created" people in motion. This ambivalence is implicit in the narrator's thrill and fear that the Mexicans will revolt:

> Their blackness was inchoate, with a dagger of white light in it. And in the inchoate blackness the blood-lust might arise, out of the sediment of the uncreated past.
> Uncreated, half-created, such a people was at the mercy of old black influences that lay in a sediment at the bottom of them. While they were quiet, they were gentle and kindly, with a sort of limp naïveté. But when anything shook them at the depths, the black clouds would arise, and they were gone again in the old grisly passions of death, blood-lust, incarnate hate. A people incomplete, and at the mercy of old, upstarting lusts. (*PS*, 147)

Kate suffers more than anyone from this attraction and repulsion. Lawrence continually monitors the psychological effects Mexico and its people have on her. The more social the action becomes, the more Kate tries to protect her individuality. In this and other respects, Kate has a great deal in common with Aaron, Lilly, and Somers. They have left Europe for the same reason: "Over in England, in Ireland, in Europe, Kate had heard the *consummatum est* of her own spirit. It was finished, in a kind of death agony. But still this heavy continent of dark-souled death was more than she could bear" (*PS*, 52). In Europe "the flow of life [. . .] had bro-

Revolution and Retreat 129

ken," and that flow could not be rekindled for Aaron, Lilly, or Somers. Kate turns to the Mexicans because, unlike the whites, they are less committed to "the cog-wheel machine of the world." At the same time, Lawrence repeatedly describes them as half-created, incomplete; only the reborn Mexican gods could raise them out of the mud.

Lawrence was attracted to the "uncreated" quality of the Mexicans, a token of their relative nonexposure to the poison of "the white Anti-Christ of Charity, and socialism, and politics, and reform." These were all the positions that, Lawrence argued, would destroy Mexico as it had Europe and North America. Don Ramon describes his people as "all half and half, incoherent, part horrible, part pathetic, part good creatures. Half arrived" (*PS*, 231). Typically, Lawrence swung between these extremes: the Indians were in touch with their bodies, but this same clayey quality, reminiscent of the workers in *The Rainbow* and *Women in Love,* is not quite human: the Indian "understands soul, which is of the blood. But spirit, which is superior, and is the quality of our civilisation, this, in the mass, he darkly and barbarically repudiates. Not until he becomes an artizan or connected with machinery does the modern spirit get him" (*PS*, 127). In *Women in Love,* Lawrence identified some of these qualities with the miners, qualities that in *Plumed Serpent* are made to seem racial:

> The dark races [the narrator observes] belong to a bygone cycle of humanity. They are left behind in a gulf out of which they have never been able to climb. And on to the particular white man's levels they never will be able to climb. They can only follow as servants. [. . .]
> A people without the energy of *getting on*, how could they fail to be hopelessly exploited? They had been hopelessly and cruelly exploited for centuries. And their backbones were locked in malevolent resistance. (*PS*, 162, 163)

On the other extreme, the opposite of the Indians "who have never been able to win a soul for themselves, never been able to win themselves a nucleus, an individual integrity out of the chaos of passions and potencies and death," are the Europeans and North Americans with whom Kate unhappily identifies. For the white man, "let him bluster as he may, is hollow with misgivings about his own supremacy. Full speed ahead, then, for the débâcle" (*PS*, 162). Either the body crushes the spirit beneath it, like the Indian, or the spirit rises out of the body, as in the case of the white man. This is the great tragedy of our times. In the American conti-

130   CLASS, POLITICS, AND THE INDIVIDUAL

nent, the narrator says, "If a man arrives with a soul, the maleficent elements gradually break it, gradually, till he decomposes into ideas and mechanistic activities, in a body full of mechanical energy, but with his blood-soul dead and putrescent" (*PS*, 148). Lawrence's lifetime objective was to find a way to put these pieces back together.

Much of *Plumed Serpent* is characterized by dilemma. The white men of Europe and America "find themselves at last shut in the tomb along with their dead god and the conquered race. Which is the status quo" (*PS*, 148). Yet sooner or later, the etiolated people of Europe and the impassive Indians of Mexico threaten to do the same thing to liberated spirits like Kate. But it is not race that frightens Kate, or Lilly, Aaron, or Somers; it is the fear of being dragged down by one's own class. In the following passage, Kate experiences many of the attractions and repulsions Lawrence articulated throughout his works about his own relationship to workers. In this scene, Kate is watching the Indians who are attending a sermon given by one of the new Quetzalcoatl priests:

> Kate was at once attracted and repelled. She was attracted, almost fascinated by the strange *nuclear* power of the men in the circle. It was like a darkly glowing, vivid nucleus of new life. Repellent the strange heaviness, the sinking of the spirit into the earth, like dark water. Repellent the silent, dense opposition to the pale-faced spiritual direction.
>
> Yet here and here alone, it seemed to her, life burned with a deep new fire. The rest of life, as she knew it, seemed wan, bleached, and sterile. The pallid wanness and weariness of her world! And here, the dark, ruddy figures in the glare of a torch [. . .] surely this was a new kindling of mankind!
>
> She knew it was so. Yet she preferred to be on the fringe, sufficiently out of contact. She could not bear to come into actual contact. (*PS*, 133)

A principal feature of *Plumed Serpent* is this ambivalence: the hope that these vital, uncorrupted bodies will rekindle mankind, and the dread of being swamped by them, the fear of having one's soul buried beneath a class and a race that is largely indifferent about and unconscious of itself. But that Lawrence should have gone from the rabble of Europe to the snakelike savages of Mexico is not so paradoxical. The real conflict in *Plumed Serpent* is found in Lawrence's (Kate's) battle with himself, his attempt to express and resolve antithetical needs. "You would always fight. You would

Revolution and Retreat 131

fight with yourself, if you were alone in the world" (*PS*, 471), a character tells Kate. She rejects the same thing Lawrence did: the attempt to reduce mankind to a set of principles. Like Lawrence, Kate does not trust people en masse and fears for her own individuality; she trusts a few friends, never a class. As a result, for the most part she does not participate in the revolution that surrounds her, while agonizing over her unwillingness to commit herself. Her aloofness is the source of her continual ambivalence toward Mexico, the Indians, and her lover, Cipriano. In her memoirs, Frieda Lawrence described Lawrence's own class estrangement:

> [Lawrence] was born into the working class. He knew the working class with a basic knowledge, their immediate response to all that went on around them, their warmhearted generosity and their incapacity to abstract and to really think. This last was his tragedy, that they could not think or follow him; primarily he wrote for them, because he loved them. [. . .] though he had left the working class, he did not belong to any other.[5]

Believing that workers will ultimately betray one's trust is characteristic of Kate also as she struggles to find her place, first in Europe, then in Mexico.

Through Kate, Lawrence boldly raised and then parodied the fundamental political questions of his age, though he often couched his efforts in religious or mystical language. In the twentieth century these issues are still relevant. In two revolutionary countries, Ireland and then Mexico, Kate dares assert her belief that "every man and every woman alike is founded on the individual" (*PS*, 426), and that she must "hold herself up, in the proud old assertion: *My blood is my own. Noli me tangere*" (*PS*, 457). At first believing she "belonged to the ruling races, the clever ones," Kate begins to question racial superiority, as well as the possibility of maintaining one's individuality in a communal world:

> But back again they demanded her acquiescence to the primeval assertion: *The blood is one blood. We are one blood.* It was the assertion that swept away all individualism, and left her immersed, drowned in the grand sea of the living blood, in immediate contact with all these men and all these women. (*PS*, 457)

So *Plumed Serpent* does what no previous Lawrence novel had been able to do with such ease: ridicule the central character be-

132 CLASS, POLITICS, AND THE INDIVIDUAL

cause of her overweening pride in individuality. Certainly Ursula was never parodied in so sharp a manner as is Kate:

> The conqueress! And now she would retire to the lair of her own individuality, with the prey.
>
> Suddenly, she saw herself as men often saw her: the great cat, with its spasms of voluptuousness and its life-long lustful enjoyment of its own isolated, isolated individuality. Voluptuously to enjoy a contact. Then with a lustful feline gratification, to break the contact, and roam alone in the sense of power. Each time, to seize a sort of power, purring upon her own isolated individuality. (*PS*, 480)

Never before had Lawrence so nearly balanced opposing claims: freeing oneself from community and politics while showing the radical need for such involvement; pulling back from and even despising the dark, savage race of Indians and simultaneously declaring that they alone could save the white, "ruling" race from itself. Wanting both to excoriate and to save mankind, Kate flees the Irish nationalist movement, only to fall into the social upheaval of Mexico. Kate is convulsed by these antithetical drives up to the last line in the novel. When Cipriano begs Kate to remain in Mexico as his wife, she responds as much to him as to her relationship with Mexico generally. His words strike her as "so soft, so soft-tongued, of the soft, wet, hot blood, that she shivered a little. 'You won't let me go!' she said to him" (*PS*, 487). The final line of the novel, like the major portion of it, is deliberately ambiguous. Kate's question is framed as an exclamation. She wants to stay—almost as much as she wants to leave.

In many respects *Plumed Serpent* was Lawrence's most inventive, most ambitious attempt to get the world to listen to him through his craft. It was also the most intentionally chaotic of his major works. For probably the last time in his major fiction, Lawrence presented a near-epic canvas, on which battle all his antithetical ideas about society, politics, and the individual. He argued in his novel that socialism was on the agenda in Mexico, even though he himself argued bitterly against political solutions. He felt that Mexico needed a spiritual or religious rebirth, but on a number of occasions Kate, one of the three ruling gods, is fearful of what this mythical religion might portend: "The re-evoked past is frightening, and if it be re-evoked to overwhelm the present, it is fiendish. Kate felt a real terror of the sound of a tom-tom. It seemed to beat straight on her solar plexus, to make her sick" (*PS*, 366). The religious-mystical aspect of *Plumed Serpent* provides by

Revolution and Retreat   133

far the most jarring contradiction of the work. In an essay on Melville's *Typee and Omoo*, Lawrence warned that Western civilization "can't go back to the savages: not a strike. We can be in sympathy with them. We can take a great curve in their direction, onwards. But we cannot turn the current of our life backwards, back towards their soft warm twilight and uncreate mud" (*S*, 137). Yet the central characters in *Plumed Serpent* try to do just this by turning a secular state into a mythical-religious one, handing the state over to three gods, one of them a European woman. "We have to go on, on, on, even if we must smash a way ahead" (*S*, 138), Lawrence wrote in the Melville essay. "The world ought *not* to be a harmonious loving place. It ought to be a place of fierce discord and intermittent harmonies: which it is" Melville, Lawrence concluded, "was, at the core, a mystic and idealist. Perhaps so am I. And he stuck to his ideal guns. I abandon mine" (*S*, 143). Of the various aspects of *Plumed Serpent* that contribute to its "fierce discords," the novel's mystical elements dominate.

Lawrence used myth and mysticism to harmonize the conflicts of class and social revolution, rich and poor, individual and community, church and state, body and spirit, and politics and spiritualism. The idealist in Lawrence intended his characters to "turn their backs on the cog-wheel world. Not to look out any more on to that horrible machine of the world" (*PS*, 114), to do without "industrialized" reasoning. Mysticism proved to be an idealistic device that was hardly satisfying, least of all to the principal character. When she finds herself speaking mystically, Kate

> was surprised at herself, suddenly using this language. But her weariness and her sense of devastation had been so complete, that the Other Breath in the air and the bluish dark power in the earth had become, almost suddenly, more real to her than so-called reality. (*PS*, 119).

In his search for harmony, Lawrence was led, as in *Rainbow*, into mysticism. In *Plumed Serpent* he raised it to an ideological substitute for politics, since he could accept neither a bourgeois nor a socialist state. But *Plumed Serpent* cannot resolve the contradiction between reality and mysticism any more than *Rainbow* could. Kate—rather like the novel as a whole—is caught between Lawrence's fear of radical politics and his consciousness of the futility of religion in the twentieth century replacing the secular state.

The Plumed Serpent represents the end of Lawrence's efforts to present a metaphysic for the future. *The Plumed Serpent* was pub-

134   CLASS, POLITICS, AND THE INDIVIDUAL

lished in 1926, and in December of that year, the first of the three *Lady Chatterley* novels was written. Thereafter, Lawrence's theme of man's struggle between the poles of privacy and community and his attempts to radically reorder society are gradually muted. The canvases of Lawrence's later works are less historical in scope, much more private. *Aaron's Rod, Kangaroo,* and *Plumed Serpent* raised many themes that thereafter Lawrence dropped from his few remaining novels. Unlike Lady Chatterley and her lovers in the three versions, the "leadership" novels are rather audacious in their approach to family, marriage, and interpersonal relationships. In these works, the main characters seek ties to people and to society beyond the limitations of any one-to-one relationship. From Aaron to Kate, marriage and family alone do not compensate for the search for a wider social involvement, even if that experience finally proves to be unsatisfactory. These characters go beyond marriage and even romance to probe the social world. By contrast, *Rainbow* and *Women in Love* conclude with one man and one woman against the world. The assorted socialists, fascists, anarchists, or "social mystics" in *Aaron's Rod, Kanagaroo,* and *Plumed Serpent* represent obviously flawed solutions, but Lawrence did show that given the limitations or poverty of personal and political relationships of the time, it was impossible to retreat into a wholly private world; such did not exist. In a book published the same year as *Aaron's Rod, Fantasia of the Unconscious,* Lawrence made clear his commitment that we had to get "back to the great unison of manhood in passionate *purpose*," that this purpose was "not like sex," since "sex is always individual":

> We have got to get back to the great purpose of manhood, a passionate unison in actively making a world. This is a real commingling of many. And in such a commingling we forfeit the individual. In the commingling of sex we are alone with *one* partner. It is an individual affair, there is no superior or inferior. But in the commingling of a passionate purpose, each individual sacredly abandons his individual. In the living faith of his soul, he surrenders his individuality to the great urge which is upon him. (*PF,* 144)

Two antithetical voices are present in these novels: the tumult of angry workers, peasants, and Indians—the voice of collective man—and the cry of the individual. Although characters like Aaron, Somers, and Kate hold stage center, the other voices are just as real. The crowd and the individual are the antinomies that

Revolution and Retreat 135

dominate these novels. That Lawrence views this tension as inevitable is evident: whereas Birkin and Ursula may have fought against the encroachment of the masses, the leadership novels unquestionably acknowledge the reality of society. This sentiment is made explicit in one of Lawrence's last works, *Apocalypse,* first published in 1931. In this work, Lawrence listed a six-point credo, "important points," he called them, "missed by Christian doctrine and Christian thought. Christian fantasy alone has grasped them." Two of these points provided much of the thematic material for *Aaron's Rod, Kangaroo,* and *Plumed Serpent:*

> No man is or can be a pure individual. The mass of men have only the tiniest touch of individuality: if any. The mass of men live and move, think and feel collectivity, and have practically no individual emotions, feelings or thoughts at all. They are fragments of the collective or social consciousness. It has always been so. And will always be so. [. . .] To have an ideal for the individual which regards only his individual self and ignores his collective self is in the long run fatal. To have a creed of individuality which denies the reality of the hierarchy makes at last for anarchy. (*A,* 122, 123)

Lawrence ended *Apocalypse,* perhaps his last statement on the great theme of society and the individual, with a magnificent shock of recognition:

> My soul knows that I am part of the human race, my soul is an organic part of the great human soul, as my spirit is part of my nation. In my own very self, I am part of my family. There is nothing of me that is alone and absolute except my mind, and we shall find that the mind has no existence by itself, it is only the glitter of the sun on the surface of the waters.
>
> So that my individualism is really an illusion. I am part of the great whole, and I can never escape. But I *can* deny my connections, break them, and become a fragment. Then I am wretched.
>
> What we want is to destroy our false, inorganic connections, especially those related to money, and re-establish the living organic connections, with the cosmos, the sun and earth, with mankind and nation and family. (*A,* 126)

If *Aaron's Rod, Kangaroo,* and *Plumed Serpent* can be read in light of this statement—that one's individualism is, finally, a grand illusion, that we are part of the great whole from which there is no escape—then it is possible to say the author was testing the potential as well as the limitations of the characters who wanted both to

136   CLASS, POLITICS, AND THE INDIVIDUAL

lead other men as well as to be left alone. Lawrence experimented with the possibility that man might shun politics to become more fully human, yet these novels are deeply, urgently political. They show a mosaic of the individual and social movements. The assertion of the individual and the demands of society and of the masses of people cannot, these books illustrate, be regarded as wholly separate claims. *Aaron's Rod, Kangaroo,* and *Plumed Serpent* are complex political works because they show to what extent community and the individual, each with its own dynamism, are inextricably bound together. In a sense, these novels are also radical: they express a warning to the ruling classes of Europe and America, to those with property and political power. This was a warning he made clear in his essay, "The Death of a Porcupine," written the same year as *Plumed Serpent:*

> We are losing vitality: losing it rapidly. Unless we seize the torch of inspiration, and drop our moneybags, the moneyless will be kindled by the flames, and they will consume us like old rags.
> We are losing vitality, owing to money and money-standards. The torch in the hands of the moneyless will set our house on fire, and burn us to death, like sheep in a flaming corral. (*Ph* 2, 474)

Although the loudest voices we hear in these books are characters who speak for Lawrence and voice his own doubts about social involvement, they are heard in contrast to the great background sounds of the multitudes with neither money nor property.

Notes

1. Georg Lukács, *The Meaning of Contemporary Realism,* trans. John Mander and Necke Mander (London: Merlin Press, 1963), p. 64.
2. Ibid., p. 74.
3. Mary Freeman, *D. H. Lawrence: A Basic Study of His Ideas* (New York: Universal Library, Grosset and Dunlop, 1955), p. 205.
4. In an 8 October 1921 letter, quoted without source, in John Worthen, *D. H. Lawrence and the Idea of the Novel* (Totowa: Rowman and Littlefield, 1979), p. 118.
5. Frieda Lawrence, "D. H. Lawrence, the Failure," in *D. H. Lawrence: A Collection of Criticism,* ed. Leo Hamalian (New York: McGraw-Hill, 1973), p. 17.

4

Radical Commitment to Eros: *The First Lady Chatterley, John Thomas and Lady Jane,* and *Lady Chatterley's Lover*

Within a span of nearly thirteen months, Lawrence finished three distinct versions of his *Lady Chatterley* novel. *The First Lady Chatterley,* begun in mid-October 1926 and finished in December, was originally published in 1944 in the United States. *John Thomas and Lady Jane,* begun in December 1926 and finished in February of the following year, was first published in an Italian translation in 1952. *Lady Chatterley's Lover* was written between December 1927 and early January 1928. It was privately printed in July 1928.

The similarities and differences between these novels offer unique insight into the conflicting themes with which Lawrence grappled during the last five years of his life. The progression from the first to the third version illustrates many of the lifelong tensions that dominated Lawrence's novels: class, politics, the individual, and sex. The wide range of differences among the three novels also reveals the extent to which Lawrence was undecided about the role of the individual in society and the extent to which the individual could or should participate in shaping his own social future. In a letter in 1925 to Mabel Dodge Luhan, Lawrence referred to some of these conflicts as the "introvert, extrovert question" (*CL,* 778), a phrase that has much to do with the development and change of the characterizations in these novels.

By 1926, Lawrence had explored many of the concerns that figure in *The First Lady Chatterley,* in particular that of class strug-

137

138   CLASS, POLITICS, AND THE INDIVIDUAL

gle and the role of the individual. In *Aaron's Rod, Kangaroo,* and *Plumed Serpent,* Lawrence acknowledged that he was of two minds about the value of political activity and the sanctity of the individual. But by the time he wrote *The First Lady Chatterley,* Lawrence wanted, he said, to meet not upon a social or purely physical or spiritual ground, but "upon the third ground, the holy ground." In this letter to Rolf Gardiner, Lawrence described his disenchantment with the social, idealistic, and intellectual world. Although his message echoes Birkin's in *Women in Love,* Birkin's misanthropism is gone. Tenderness was the "holy ground" Lawrence wished to create in his *Chatterley* novels:

> One needs to establish a fuller relationship between oneself and the universe, and between oneself and one's fellow man and fellow woman. It doesn't mean cutting out the "brothers-in-Christ" business simply: it means expanding it into a full relationship, where there can be also physical and passional meeting, as there used to be in the old dances and rituals. We have to know how to go out and meet one another, upon the third ground, the holy ground. You see, you yourself go out intensely in the spirit, as it were, to meet some fellow men. But another part of yourself, the fighting and the passionate part, never issues [. . .] from its shell. [. . .] We need to come forth and meet in the essential physical self, on some third holy ground. (*CL,* 940–41)

Lawrence began his *Chatterley* novels with these sentiments.

The year was 1926, the year the British miners sparked the great General Strike. Rather than rejoice that the colliers, whom he had so often regretted acted like whipped dogs, were fighting back, Lawrence found the strike very depressing. The upsurge in class struggle reinforced his intentions to meet on some ground, passionate and physical but not socially militant. In a letter to S. S. Koteliansky, Lawrence described his visit to the Midlands in September 1926: "This strike had done a lot of damage—and there is a lot of misery—families living on bread and margarine and potatoes—nothing more. The women have turned into fierce communists—you would hardly believe your eyes. It feels like a different place—not pleasant all" (*CL,* 937). Later that same year, Lawrence told Gardiner that the strike "was like a spear through one's heart. I tell you, we'd better buck up and do something for England to come, for they've pushed the spear through the side of *my* England" (*CL,* 952). The strike distressed Lawrence: it was violent and it centered around the distribution of property and money, materialism that he despised. The violence of class conflict affected

Radical Commitment to Eros

Lawrence enormously. He had given up his earlier interest in revolution. "The strike is over, apparently," he wrote to Koteliansky in May 1926. "I'm very glad. Myself, I'm scared of a class war in England. It would be the beginning of the end of all things" (*CL*, 912).

In large measure, Lawrence began his *Chatterley* works with the fears and resentments these struggles in England evoked for him. He had often chided the British people for their "smallness, meanness, fathomless ugliness, combined with a sort of chapel-going respectability." Lawrence wrote this description as part of an unfinished autobiography he began in late October 1927. In this "Autobiographical Fragment," Lawrence compared the colliers of his father's generation with those of the present:

> Now it seems so different. The colliers of today are the men of my generation, lads I went to school with. I find it hard to believe. They were rough, wild lads. They are not rough, wild men. The board-school, the Sunday-school, the Band of Hope, and, above all, their mothers got them under. Got them under, made them tame. Made them sober, conscientious, and decent. Made them good husbands. When I was a boy, a collier who was a good husband was an exception to the rule, and while the women with bad husbands pointed him out as a shining example, they also despised him a little, as a petticoat man. (*Ph 1*, 817)

Lawrence was less interested in the colliers' apparent marital domesticity than he was in their social passivity. He feared revolution, but he was clearly attracted to the social unconventionality of his father's generation. When Lawrence began his three *Chatterley* novels, he wanted something other than the less-than-pious, rebellious collier. He wished to create a smaller, more private world than the explosive, militant working-class world he was witness to in 1926. "I feel," Lawrence wrote to Gardiner, "how very hard it is to get anything *real* going." He continued:

> Until a few men have an active feeling that the world, the social world, can offer little or nothing any more; and until there can be some tangible desire for a new sort of relationship between people, one is bound to beat about the bush. It is difficult not to fall into a sort of preciosity and a sort of faddism. (*CL*, 940)

Although Lawrence wanted to resolve the class warfare raging in Europe after the First World War, resolve it if possible with an

140   CLASS, POLITICS, AND THE INDIVIDUAL

intimacy based on physical and spiritual union, he had almost equally strong urgings pulling him elsewhere. Between 1926 and 1928, before his rapidly declining health, British censorship of his novel, and his paintings began to dominate his correspondence, Lawrence's letters were characterized by two fundamentally antithetical concerns. The first is the weltschmerz already alluded to—which accounted for Lawrence's departure from England as early as 1922, thereafter never to stay in any country for longer than a year. By August 1926, when Lawrence made his last visit to England, he wanted desperately to escape any social involvement. In a letter to E. H. Brewster in 1926, Lawrence wrote:

> I am getting weary, and wearier, of the outside world. I want the world from the inside, not from the outside. Which doesn't mean, for me, killing desire and anger. Greed, lust, yes! But desire and anger are from God. Give me anything which is from God, desire or anger or communion of saints, or even hurts. But nothing any more of the dreariness and the mechanism of man. (*CL*, 905)

Based on this sentiment, Lawrence set out to write a book he intended to call *Tenderness*.

Another Lawrence is revealed in his letters, however, one whose concerns emerge most strongly in the first and second, though not in the third *Lady Chatterley* novel. While he longed for the private, intimately shared life, Lawrence also ached for a scrap with the social forces he detested—industrial capitalism and the sexual, psychic, and economic injuries it imposed. The triad of novels beginning with *Aaron's Rod* shows Lawrence's willingness to embrace even chaos if necessary to avoid the trap of cynicism and social isolation. In 1922, *Aaron's Rod* was published, and Lawrence left the West because he was "so tired of Europe." He thought he might experience peace and dharma in Buddhist Ceylon; but Lawrence discovered he was more interested in a good social fight than in transcendental peace. This was the "other" Lawrence. In a letter to E. H. Brewster from Ceylon in January 1922, Lawrence described this interest:

> More and more I feel that meditation and the inner life are not my aim, but some sort of action and strenuousness and pain and frustration and struggling through. All the things you don't believe in I do. And the goal is not that men should become serene as Buddha or as gods, but that the unfleshed gods should become men in battle. God-made man is the goal. The gods are uneasy till they can become men. And the

Radical Commitment to Eros

fight and the sorrow and the loss of blood, and even the influenzas and the headache are part of the fight and the fulfilment. (*CL*, 681)

Thereafter, Lawrence's letters are dominated by two contending concerns. The first was to dissociate himself from any group whatsoever, and to pursue his craft, in particular painting, which he had just seriously begun. The second was to leave off being an introvert. "A *pure* extrovert is insane and a destructive influence," he wrote in 1924. "So is a pure introvert," he warned Mabel Luhan:

> You are too much an introvert. Then learn, and humbly learn to be sufficiently an extrovert, so that you may have a balance. Otherwise it's all no good. You've got to curb your introverted pride, first and foremost. One's pride should be in one's wholeness, not in an intensification of one's own partiality. You pride yourself on your intense power of *drawing-in* to yourself. But in the end, this power is *your* destruction. If you want to destroy yourself in this way, well and good. If you don't, you must quite humbly learn to go forth and give. (*CL*, 778–79)

In this letter, Lawrence chided his one-time hostess and the model for "The Woman Who Rode Away" for the traits he recognized in himself and that he strove for so many years to overcome.

Despite his negative encounters with socialist and fascist movements in Italy and Australia, Lawrence was appalled as much by his own social isolation as he was by class warfare. "If being an introvert means always drawing in, in, in to yourself," he wrote to Mabel Luhan, "and not going bravely out, and giving yourself, then for God's sake wash windows also and go out to them, if only savagely" (*CL*, 777).

During the war years and immediately afterwards, Lawrence had good reason to consider himself a fugitive from society. *Women in Love* reflected his shellshocked reaction to the war in progress. Birkin thinks that in the privacy of his relationship with Ursula he can dig individual-sized trenches. The books that Lawrence published after the war, *Lost Girl* (1921), *Aaron's Rod* (1922), and *Kangaroo* (1923), portray characters in flight. But Lawrence's trip to the United States in March 1924 seemed to bring out the combatant in him. By July he was "sick of the farce of cosmic unity, or world unison. It may exist in the abstract—but not elsewhere" (*CL*, 796). Perhaps he was goaded by what he said was the mechanical willfulness of America. At least for the moment, Lawrence was ready to cast aside the pretense that class or

142 CLASS, POLITICS, AND THE INDIVIDUAL

social differences could be sidestepped. Now, instead of attempting to avoid conflict, to avoid rocking an already listing social ship, Lawrence welcomed a war with society. He said he wanted a fight—something Aaron, Lilly, and, finally, Somers spent a great deal of time trying to avoid:

> what is it to me, world unison and peace and all that? I am essentially a fighter—to wish me peace is bad luck—except the fighter's peace. And I have known many things, that may never be unified [. . .] don't talk to me of unison. No more unison among man than among wild animals—coyotes and chipmunks and porcupines and deer and rattlesnakes. They all live in these hills—in the unison of avoiding one another. As for *willing* the world into better shape—better chaos a thousand times than any "perfect" world. Why, you can't even have a "perfect" camp on a Bucks common—Blarney!
> To me, chaos doesn't matter so much as abstract, which is mechanical order. To me it is life to feel the white ideas and the "oneness" crumbling into a thousand pieces, and all sorts of wonder coming through. [. . .] I hate "oneness," it's a mania. (*CL*, 796)

Both *Plumed Serpent* and *The First Lady Chatterley* reflect Lawrence's wish to "take up a hatchet, not a dummy teat of commiseration" to "smash a few big holes in European suburbanity, let in a little fresh air" (*CL*, 800). The fascist ideology that Rolf Gardiner continually dangled in front of Lawrence certainly got the latter's combative spirit up; anything short of radical was insufficient:

> It's courage that we want, fresh air, and not suffused sentiments. Even the stars are stale, that way. If one is going to act, in words, one should go armed to the teeth, and fire carefully. [. . .]
> If it's going to be Youth, then let it be Youth on the warpath, not wandervogeling and piping imitation nature tunes to the taste of a cake of milk chocolate, and pitying itself and "all other unfortunates." To the rubbish heap with all unfortunates. A great *merde!* to all latter-day Joan-of-Arcism. God, God, God, if there *be* any Youth in Europe, let them rally and kick the bottom of all this elderly bunk. Not snivel or feel helpless. What's the good being hopeless, so long as one has a hobnailed boot to kick with? *Down with the Poor in Spirit!* A war! But the Subtlest most intimate warfare. Smashing the face of what one *knows* is rotten. (*CL*, 801)

Typically the language is more armed to the teeth than is the practical solution; nor, in fact, is the problem itself defined. Lawrence

Radical Commitment to Eros

was extreme in his hatred of bourgeois democracy, industrialism, and plutocracy, but any political solution eluded him.

The *Lady Chatterley* novels come out of this period of extremes: feeling daunted by the wreckage of industrialism, war, and revolution; wanting to reconcile mankind by offering tenderness and one-to-one intimacy; and feeling isolated and trying to get back into an appropriate collective fray. The letter Lawrence wrote to Dr. Trigant Burrow in 1927 is indicative of the dilemma Parkin (the original gamekeeper) and Mellors find themselves in: simultaneously threatened by society and oppressed by their isolation:

> It is our being cut off that is our ailment, and out of this ailment everything bad arises. [. . .] Myself, I suffer badly from being so cut off. But what is one to do? One can't link up with the social unconscious. At times, one is *forced* to be essentially a hermit. I don't want to be. But anything else is either a personal tussle or a money tussle: sickening: except, of course, just for ordinary acquaintance, which remains acquaintance. One has no real human relations—that is so devastating. (*CL*, 993)

In fact, the major differences that exist among the three versions are a result of a pull toward introversion and a pull toward extroversion. The structure of his novels seems to follow the pattern of his letters: the major social issues of the day are raised and then quickly put aside. When Lawrence's political friends got too persistent, Lawrence reasserted his privacy. "There needs a centre of silence," he wrote to Gardiner, "and a heart of darkness" (*CL*, 950).

At the same time, during the thirteen months he wrote the *Chatterley* works, Lawrence referred continually to the system of private property he said had to be eliminated. He was of two minds about what role workers might play, if any, in bringing a new society to pass. But Lawrence was never equivocal about property owners, the Sir Cliffords of the world: "I have absolutely no basic sympathy with people of 'assured income,'" he wrote in June 1927. "All words become a lie, in their mouths, in their ears also. I *loathe* rich people" (*CL*, 984). Perhaps more than any other letter Lawrence wrote during these months, the one to Dr. Burrow in July 1927 best captures how much Lawrence wanted to be socially committed, and how little he felt he could be:

> What ails me is the absolute frustration of my primeval societal instinct. The hero illusion starts with the individualist illusion, and all

144   CLASS, POLITICS, AND THE INDIVIDUAL

resistances ensue. I think societal instinct much deeper than sex instinct—and societal repression much more devastating. There is no repression of the sexual individual comparable to the repression of the societal man in me, by the individual ego, my own and everybody else's. I am weary even of my own individuality, and simply nauseated by other people's.[. . .] What a beastly word, *societal!* (*CL*, 989–98)

The *Chatterley* works come out of these conflicting and often contradictory pressures. The fact that he wrote the novel three ways reflects these divergent perspectives. However, recent criticism of the *Chatterley* novels ignores this fact. Rarely are the three versions discussed as the overlapping works they are. Critic after critic assumes Lawrence was making a particular statement—usually a sexual one—in each of the three *Chatterley* novels. Yet Lawrence explicitly warned against finding thematic handles in his works to hang onto. In a successful novel, he wrote in an essay called "The Novel," "there's always a tom-cat, black tom-cat that pounces on the white dove of the Word, if the dove doesn't watch it; and there is a banana-skin to trip on" (*Ph* 2, 418). " 'Refrain from hooking on!' says the novel" (*Ph* 2, 425). The *Lady Chatterley* works are rewarding precisely because the author never hooked on to a single thesis; compared to *John Thomas and Lady Jane* and *Lady Chatterley's Lover, The First Lady Chatterley* is the black tom-cat.

The First Lady Chatterley: A Commitment to Political Radicalism

Lawrence began *The First Lady Chatterley* novel in 1926, the year he left England for good. In August, the Lawrences left for Scotland. From then on, until his death on 2 March 1930, his works are characterized by curious blend of anger, determination, and hopelessness. He expressed certain sentiments that he declared to be revolutionary, though he spent his remaining years commuting among Italy, Germany, and France, thereby guaranteeing his outsider status. He seemed more determined than ever that England needed to undergo a great social upheaval, but he was modest about his role in that change, occasionally admitting his own inability to judge in those matters. The *Chatterley* books reflect this tentativeness about where to go, what to do. However, the novels do present clearly enough the social and political issue of the times.

Radical Commitment to Eros

The fact that the setting for the three versions is England, including the mining areas of the Midlands, is indicative of Lawrence's on-again, off-again belief that the British workers would have a voice in England's future, a faith that he articulated in this letter to Earl Brewster in August 1926:

> Curiously, I like England again, now I am up in my own regions. It braces me up: and there seems a queer, odd sort of potentiality in the people, especially the common people. One feels in them some odd, unaccustomed sort of plasm twinkling and nascent. They are not finished. And they have a funny sort of purity and gentleness, and at the same time, unbreakableness, that attracts one. (*CL*, 933)

In 1928, the year *Lady Chatterley's Lover* was published, Lawrence began a series of essays on sex, the family, marriage, and society. In one of these articles called "The State of Funk," he put forward many of the concerns on which the *Chatterley* works were based:

> What is the matter with the English, that they are so scared of everything? They are in a state of blue funk, and they behave like a lot of mice when somebody stamps on the floor. They are terrified about money, finance, about ships, about war, about Labour, about Bolshevism, and funniest of all, they are scared stiff of the printed word. Now this is a very strange and humiliating state of mind, in a people which has always been so dauntless. And, for the nation, it is a very dangerous state of mind. When a people falls into a state of funk, then God help it. Because mass funk leads some time or other to mass panic, and then—one can only repeat, God help us.
>
> There is, of course, a certain excuse for fear. The time of change is upon us. The need for change has taken hold of us. We are changing, we have got to change. (*Ph 2*, 565)

"Change in the whole social system is inevitable not merely because conditions change—though partly for that reason—but because people themselves change," he concluded (*Ph 2*, 567). This is a central theme in the first *Chatterley*. With his sights set a good bit lower than in *Plumed Serpent*, Lawrence began *The First Lady Chatterley*, not to reorder society, but to describe the agony of positive individual change in a world fettered by class hatreds and social exploitation.

> The change [. . .] inside the individual is my real concern [Lawrence wrote]. The great social change interests me and troubles me, but it is

146 CLASS, POLITICS, AND THE INDIVIDUAL

not my field. I know a change is coming—and I know we must have a more generous, more human system based on the life values and not on the money values. That I know. But what steps to take I don't know. Other men know better. (*Ph 2*, 567)

Other men know better. This self-doubt caused Lawrence to move away from the overt politics of the leadership novels. In the *Chatterley* works, no one tries to be heroic, let alone provide a social program, as did Kangaroo or Struthers. Lawrence began to feel that social and economic relationships were a bit too complex to justify the militance of such men as Cooley, Struthers, Don Ramon, and General Cipriano. In a letter to Witter Bynner in 1928, Lawrence wrote that he was finished with militant heroes:

The hero is obsolete, and the leader of men is a back number. After all, at the back of the hero is the militant ideal: and the militant ideal, or the ideal militant, seems to me also a cold egg. We're sort of sick of all forms of militarism and militantism [. . .] the leader-cum-follower relationship is a bore. And the new relationship will be some sort of tenderness, sensitive, between men and men and men and women, and not the one up one down, lead on I follow, *ich dien* sort of business. So you see I'm becoming a lamb at last. (*CL*, 1045)

And in his review of *Pedro de Valdivia* by R. B. Cunninghame Graham, Lawrence wrote:

Men of action are usually deadly failures in the long run. Their precious energy makes them uproot the tree of life, and leave it to wither, and their stupidity makes them proud of it. [. . .] We, who suffer from the bright deeds of the men of action of the past, may well keep an eye on the "tall fellows of their hands" of our own day. (*Ph 1*, 358, 359)

For perhaps the first time in his major novels, Lawrence tried something different with the *Chatterley* works: the main character neither flees in disgust from society, nor tried heroically to lead it. The gamekeeper in the first two versions has few of the elitist qualities that characterize most of Lawrence's protagonists since *Rainbow*. In *Chatterley* 1 and 2, Lawrence tried to integrate the needs of the individual with the demands of the community, something he had suggested almost ten years earlier in his essay called "Education of the People":

A real individual has a spark of danger in him, a menace to society. Quench this spark and you quench the individuality, you obtain a

Radical Commitment to Eros 147

social unit, not an integral man. All modern progress has tended, and still tends, to the production of quenched social units: dangerless beings, ideal creatures.

On the other hand, by the over-development of the individualistic qualities, you produce a disintegration of all society. This was the Greek danger, as the quenching of the individual in the social unit was the Roman danger.

You must have a harmony and an inter-relation between the two modes. Because, though man is first and foremost an individual being, yet the very accomplishing of his individuality rests upon his fulfillment in social life. If you isolate an individual you deprive him of his life: if you leave him no isolation you deprive him of himself. And there it is! Life consists in the interaction between a man and his fellows, from the individual, integral love in each. (*Ph 1,* 613–14)

This sentiment is expressed in the gamekeeper Parkin. He is his own man, surely, but he identifies strongly with his class; and is under no illusions that he is exempt from social necessity. In many ways the movement from the first to the third version of *Lady Chatterley* typifies a salient feature in all of Lawrence's works: a portrayal of a world characterized by class differences and a gradual retreat from this position. By the third version, Mellors argues that political action is an inadequate response to the social paralysis of capitalism. Sex is seen as politically subversive, a force that rejuvenates the individual at a time when society must be rejected, a notion Lawrence worked into *Rainbow, Women in Love, Lost Girl,* and *Plumed Serpent.* Taken as a whole, the three versions demonstrate how, over a lifetime, Lawrence integrated his great themes: sex, politics, class, the individual, materialism, and spirituality.

Of these, class predominates in *The First Lady Chatterley.* In this novel, unlike the next two, all roads lead back to a social-economic system. Parkin and Sir Clifford are identified primarily by their class. Whereas *Lady Chatterley's Lover* concentrated on the sterility of the mental life, which Lawrence argued had replaced the reality of the body, *The First Lady Chatterley* speaks of a social system turned to stone, an outmoded capitalist society that has outlived its usefulness and is responsible for the estrangement between men and women.

Not since *Lost Girl,* published five years earlier, can one find a Lawrence novel in which the material conditions of life so determine the actions and attitudes of the major characters. In the earlier work, Alvina Houghton leaves her family, her profession, and,

148 CLASS, POLITICS, AND THE INDIVIDUAL

finally, her country to escape "being worn-down by the regular machine-friction of our average and mechanical days" (*LG,* 98). Alvina is in flight from her father's class—the turn-of-the-century British bourgeoisie. Everyone she sees—her parents, governess, friends, and lovers—is slowly being smothered by the materialism of this class. To escape, she marries an Italian peasant and leaves England for good. *The First Lady Chatterley* shares the dominant sentiment of this work: England has evolved into two rigidly opposed classes; between them no reconciliation seems possible. From the first to the last page Wragby Hall is described as a tomb. Unlike other works in which Lawrence took major social issues—class, revolution, and war—and metamorphosed them into psychological ones, in *The First Lady Chatterley* he faced these issues squarely, without drawing back from them. In the third work, Tommy Dukes sees social conflict, in particular the Russian Revolution, as the "forcing" of ideas on to life, "forcing one's deepest instincts; our deepest feelings we force according to certain ideas. We drive ourselves with a formula, like a machine" (*LCL,* 39).

On the other hand, in *Chatterley* 1, a social problem is consistently responded to with a social solution. Duncan, a declassed individual (as Lawrence sometimes saw himself), articulates a central theme of this book. Despite his own disappointments in Soviet communism, "I can see," Duncan tells Connie, "the working people will *have* to do something about it sooner or later" (*FLC,* 222). What the English really want, Duncan continues, is "contact! Some sort of passionate human contact among themselves." Mellors says the same thing but feels that sexual warm-heartedness can bring this contact about. In the first *Chatterley,* Lawrence remains true to the social model he set up. Duncan explains how this new order might come to pass: "Perhaps if the communists *did* smash the famous 'system' there might emerge a new relationship between men: *really* not caring about money, *really* caring for life, and the life-flow with one another" (*FLC,* 222). A few lines later Duncan reiterates this point—one not found in the third version and only tentatively suggested in the second:

> It's the system, I believe the English, a sufficient quantity of them, are weary of materialism and weary of hardening their hearts to keep it going.—No, I've hated democracy since the war. But now I see I'm wrong calling for an aristocracy. What we want is a flow of life from one to another—to release some natural flow in us that urges to be released. (*FLC,* 222)

Radical Commitment to Eros

In this statement Lawrence shows how capable he was of self-criticism and change. Duncan's words are a direct repudiation of the elitism and antidemocratic sentiment of Ursula, Birkin, Lilly, Aaron, Somers, or Don Ramon. Lawrence had come a long way indeed from his wartime statement in his essay, "The Reality of Peace":

> Let there be no humanity [the author wrote in February–March 1917]; let there be a few men. Sweet death, smash the glassy rind of humanity, as one would smash the brittle hide of the insulated bug. Smash humanity, and make an end of it. Let there emerge a few pure and single men—men who give themselves to the unknown of life and death and are fulfilled. Make an end of our unholy oneness, O death, give us to our single being. Release me from the debased social body, O death, release me at last; let me be by myself, let me be myself (*Ph 1*, 686–87).

Parkin could not represent a more antithetical view. He is the first sympathetic character who does not preach class reconciliation, who expresses no interest in getting the rich and poor together in some mystical union: "I want to stop where I am. I don't want you. I don't want nothing of yours," he tells Connie (*FLC*, 163). Workers and owners were not "in the same world an' never would be," he tells her; furthermore, class hostility is inevitable, "bound to be from the beginning" (*FLC*, 175).

Unlike Lawrence's other militants—Struthers, Cooley, Don Ramon, or Willie Houghton—Parkin genuinely identifies with workers. When Connie tells him that she wants to buy him a farm so he may escape working in a factory, Parkin makes, for Lawrence, a singular statement:

> Ay! An' t' other chaps? Would they all find women wi' money to pick 'em up an' start 'em on their own? They've got to ding at it till Doomsday, and their children after them, with no more hope in it than if they was dead. [. . .]—Ay, I should get away on a woman's money! But what about all them chaps as'll niver get away, niver, not till kingdom come an' after? What about them? (*FLC*, 204)

When Duncan intervenes for Connie, asking Parkin what is so sacred about his factory job, the gamekeeper responds, "That's another thing! I'm secretary for our men, at our works, of the Communist League. That's another thing I don't want to drop" (*FLC*, 217). And by the end of this novel, Connie herself comes almost to share Parkin's militance. Wragby Hall, she feels, is "that

150   CLASS, POLITICS, AND THE INDIVIDUAL

death-in-life." "Let the tidal wave sweep [Clifford] and all his sort away forever" (*FLC*, 231).

Unlike *Kangaroo* or *Plumed Serpent*, where Harriet and Kate provide a certain check to their husbands' radicalism, Connie joins her lover in condemning the social status quo. Instead of mistrusting social commitment, Connie escapes from the prison of absolute selfhood: "If one wanted to be so tremendously free," she thinks, "one must evaporate into nothingness. That hard little freedom of a separate, completely separated individual, that was worse than a prison. It was just a nail through one's heart" (*FLC*, 105). "Reduce" the modern man or woman "to simple individuality," the narrator comments, "to assertive personal egoism of the modern individual, and each sees in the other the enemy" (*FLC*, 197). This sentiment, together with Connie's imprecations against Wragby, conflict with the idea that through one another, through one-to-one contact, we can find salvation.

The First Lady Chatterley marks a dramatic departure from Lawrence's previous novels in another way. The leadership novels celebrate the individual while acknowledging the need to participate in a collective, social experience to retain one's humanity. A short story, "The Man Who Loved Islands," serves as a reminder to that effect. Protagonists in many of Lawrence's novels make the journey from family and social responsibility to social exile: Alvina Houghton, Birkin, Ursula, Aaron, and Lilly. Somers and Kate are more complicated insofar as they waver continually between private and public concerns. But *The First Lady Chatterley* makes an unequivocal statement about the supremacy of the "societal instinct" over the private or sexual sphere. Constance Chatterley progresses from the isolation of Wragby Hall and its well-protected woods to the outside world, including Tevershall. Approximately five months before Lawrence began *The First Lady Chatterley*, he wrote to Mabel Luhan, "I do think one ought, if one can, to remove the fight (the fight *is* essential) from the field of one's personal relationship, and put it in the impersonal field of the combat with this fixed and rotten society" (*CL*, 915). Two months later, in a letter to Rolf Gardiner, Lawrence revealed a truth about himself that explained a central ambivalence in his works and provided a motive for creating an aristocratic woman like Connie who commits herself to a political militant:

> As far as anything *matters*, I have always been very much alone, and regretted it. But I can't belong to clubs, or societies, or Freemasons, or

Radical Commitment to Eros

any other damn thing. So if there is, with you, an activity I *can* belong to, I shall'thank my stars. But, of course, I shall be wary beyond words, of committing myself. (*CL*, 928)

As always, Lawrence wanted two things at once: to be part of a movement like Parkin, but to be outside like Constance.

Because of Lawrence's ambivalence, characters make political statements they themselves are ill-prepared to carry through. In *The First Lady Chatterley*, the most articulate expression against egoism is made, ironically, by Duncan, a man for whom social action is only an abstraction. That Lawrence was still "wary beyond words" of commitment is evidenced by what happens in the second and third versions. Duncan's explanation about "what's the matter with people today" is unusually strong for a major character in Lawrence. It is, however, hard to forget that it is delivered by a wealthy man who has few social ties.

> With a paltry modern egoism, we are like grit between each other's teeth and grains of sand in each other's eyes. Each his own little ego like a grain of sand. It's not only the seed of Abraham that are like the sands of the seashore, it's everybody in the world. A whole Sahara of grains of sand, barren, egoistic little individuals who sing like sand sings, in friction: "Alleluia! Here am I! Wonderful, excellent, marvellous I!" [. . .] Myself! Myself! Myself! And the people who go about talking violets and pouring syrup over us to mix us into a sand-torte, a sand-cake, they are the foulest egoists of all, pouring the slime of their ego over me, like birdlime. (*FLC*, 195)

The distance is great between *The First Lady Chatterley*, and *Rainbow* and *Women in Love*, where statements such as Duncan's would have seemed out of place. Lawrence still valued privacy and the inviolability of the individual, but he saw the limitations of the isolated man with his "stale egoism."

John Thomas and Lady Jane: The Shift away from Radicalism

John Thomas and Lady Jane was finished in February 1927, two months after *The First Lady Chatterley* was completed. It represents a change in direction, as though Lawrence were having second thoughts about the possibility of social change in a world gone mad. Lawrence was beginning to edge away again from Parkin's belief that the ruling classes actually rule, that British industrialism

152   CLASS, POLITICS, AND THE INDIVIDUAL

was run by Clifford's class for profit. In the second *Chatterley* "the whole world [is] a madhouse, Wragby was the centre of a vast and raving lunacy" (*JT*, 16). The state is not an organ of class rule, and Lawrence now expresses a plague on all classes, as if English capitalism were a universal state of mind. *John Thomas* also has roots in *Women in Love:* the two books are dominated by conflicting extremes—order, disorder; reason, chaos, a class view of society, and a private, psychological-sexual frame of reference. Given the novel's presumption that most of society is bedlamite, characters often rage until, like Parkin and Connie, they end in uneasy exile, almost as far apart from one another at the end as they were in the beginning. The work returns to a central Lawrentian thesis: the confining relations of production, combined with a rigid class system in which master and laborer are pitted, make healthy, intimate relationships all but impossible. *The First Lady Chatterley* suggested this also but the contrast with *John Thomas* is crucial. In the first work Parkin is a communist because he thinks workers can free society through militant social change, but in the second *Chatterley* a new hopelessness is introduced. Neither Connie or Parkin seems certain of their class allegiance or the possibility of social change. Class hatred in *The First Lady Chatterley* is largely replaced by fear and uncertainty, as the following observation by Connie suggests:

> There was no longer any such thing as class. The world was one vast proletariat. Everything else had gone. The true working class was gone, as much as the honorable bourgeoisie, or the proud aristocracy. Bolshevist or Fascist, the world was proletarian, a vast homogeneous proletariat made up the whole of humanity. (*JT*, 293)

As Lawrence abandoned his theme in *The First Lady Chatterley*—that it is possible to consummate a love relationship only within the context of positive social change—the tone of the second book resembles that of *Women in Love*. British society is dying, Connie thinks, so why not deliver the coup de grace to it all, master and worker alike? The occasional nihilism of the second version contrasts sharply with the optimism of the first. In *John Thomas* Constance is frequently dominated by a hatred that has nothing in common with the social consciousness of Parkin or Lady Chatterley of *The First Lady Chatterley:*

> She longed to destroy it all, smash the whole thing to smithereens: smash up Wragby, burn it down, anything, anything to erase it and

Radical Commitment to Eros

153

wipe it out of existence. She hated it with a mad and at the same time exquisite hatred. The exquisite relief it would be if she saw it in flames, and then in ashes; and then even the blackened stones torn apart; and at last, nothing but nettles, just nettles in the place where it had been. [. . .] It would be good to be dead, if one knew the world was destroyed. But what would be the good of dying, as all the men had died in the war, and leaving the world still wagging, as foul and even fouler than before! Growing fouler every minute! Bah! Fools, to be dead, and not even able to hate it! (*JT*, 42)

In *The First Lady Chatterley*, Wragby Hall is doomed but not Tefershall. "Constance felt that the old world was doomed. Even Wragby, she felt, was doomed. The great landowners when they opened the collieries doomed their own ancestral halls. One thing pushes out another" (*FLC*, 48). At least in the working class, Connie feels, a future is struggling to be realized:

They are so terribly cut off from their own *beauty*, these people.—And yet I feel they've got it, somewhere: even when they look so ugly. But they've got something tender in them that might blossom out in generations into a lovely life. It only needs developing.—Oh, how wrong our education is! How wicked we are to them, really! (*JT*, 49–50)

Between *Women in Love* and *John Thomas* other similarities exist: Out of the wreckage of "the old thing, the dead civilization," the second Lady Chatterley and Parkin, little Birkin and Ursula, hope to salvage a private life. Very little else is worth saving, neither the "rabble" of Tevershall, nor the "sterile" flying ants of the present ant-heap," which is how Tommy Dukes refers to everyone, especially middle-class intellectuals. In *John Thomas*, Lawrence returns to the theme of *Women in Love*, namely, that physical intimacy offers the primary means of becoming human again. A great deal of Birkin's generalized antiintellectualism, antimaterialism, misanthropy, and distrust of society reemerges in the character of Constance:

She didn't want any more dead things and pale triumphs, no more engines, no more machines, no more riches and luxury. She wanted live things, only live things: grass and trees on the earth, and flowers that looked after themselves. [. . .] There *must* be life again on earth, and fewer people. There *must* be fewer people!

There must be the resurrection of the body, not for ever this tombstricken spirit creeping about. It must end. Pallid miners, creeping like caterpillars by the thousand, from under the earth! What for? It was all

154   CLASS, POLITICS, AND THE INDIVIDUAL

bodiless and ghoulish. The resurrection of the body! Even the true
Christian creed insisted on it. (*JT,* 90)

Parkin and Constance see themselves as "fugitives from the nasty
world of people" (*JT,* 94). Unlike their counterparts in the first
version, they find few distinctions between Clifford's and Parkin's
class. All men and women act predictably the same: "Gentlemen
prefer blondes, but they like bonds, especially those that pay well,
better still. And blondes prefer gentlemen" (*JT,* 106), notes the
omniscient and voluble narrator. The narrator keeps setting the
tone: Our society is insane;

> the whole process is one of helpless insanity. All the complexes that
> were ever located are swallowed up in the grand complex of helpless
> acquisitiveness, the complex of the swollen ego. It possesses almost
> every individual in every class of society in every nation on earth. It is a
> vast disease, and seems to be the special disease of our civilization or
> our epoch. If you haven't got the disease, you are abnormal. (*JT,* 106)

But *John Thomas* is not a rewrite of Lawrence's earlier novel. By
1927, Lawrence saw the futility of Birkin's isolation and he had no
wish to repeat it. Whereas Birkin spoke of annihilating both
classes, the problem for Lawrence in *John Thomas* is to "resolve
them back into a oneness" (*JT,* 113). The novel represents more a
questioning of the original gamekeeper's development as a communist organizer than it does an outright negation of what he
stood for. How can the two lovers fit into a social framework? the
book asks. Should they, in fact, even bother?

As *The First Lady Chatterley, Fantasia,* and his letters at this
time make clear, Lawrence was convinced that sexuality could be
fulfilled only when the wounds of a fragmented society were
healed. The "collective purpose" and sexual gratification cannot be
separated, he argued in his essay on the unconscious. The social
principle and "true sexual passion" are dependent on one another,
Fantasia asserts (*PF,* 145). Yet the one great social purposive activity Lawrence was witness to was the one he most feared: class
conflict and revolution. In *John Thomas,* this fear stood like Cere-
brus between the lovers, continually thwarting intimacy and passion. Parkin and Connie have a harder time than do their counterparts in the *First Chatterley* because they cannot resolve these
contradictions. They acknowledge the pervasiveness of class antagonisms, and they wish to reconcile these hatreds, but Lady

Radical Commitment to Eros

Chatterley, like Lawrence, is suspicious of both classes and can ally herself with neither:

> And again came over her her hatred of those doomed, dreadful Midlands, with all their clang of iron and their smoke of coal. But the doom was taking on a new, bristling sort of terror. In the peculiar stagnancy of the depressed conditions a strange poisonous gas seemed to be distilling. Dimly she could feel some new sort of disaster accumulating: accumulating slowly, with awful, serpentine slowness, but with peculiar cold dread. [. . .] She did not want to see it. She did not want to live through the results of English class hatred, that is so deep and still unacknowledged. If society was insane [. . .] surely this class hate was the most dangerous manifestation of the insanity! It was a hate that would go so deep, so deep. It would go to the very bottom of the human soul. And it would be so awful! (*JT,* 112–13)

Parkin and Lady Chatterley in *The First Lady Chatterley* chose, with some reservations, a side they could struggle with. In the second version, choosing sides is besides the point, since their fight seems to be against everyone. With the whole world proletarianized, with the "gentry [. . .] still masquerading on the stage," and the people beginning to howl in the audience, why turn up at the social show at all:

> [Constance] felt she belonged neither to the actors nor to the audience. She wanted to come off the stage and be in touch with the people. But once the audience had started to howl, there was no being in touch with it. And the stage, the place of the upper classes, was becoming a place of pure humiliation. What was to be done? Merely wait for the fracas? (*JT,* 113)

Parkin expresses Lawrence's own despair when he says that "with all his soul, he hated the humiliating complications of the human world" (*JT,* 118).

John Thomas concludes with many of the uncertainties of *Lady Chatterley's Lover.* In the tenderness and intimacy of the flesh, "which is so much beyond the carping of human knowledge," one's faith in life may be restored. Whereas *The First Lady Chatterley* ends on a decisive, combative note—possibly explaining why Frieda Lawrence preferred it to the other versions, with Connie's uncompromising hatred for Wragby and all that it stood for: "let the tidal wave sweep [Clifford] and all his sort away forever"—(*FLC,* 231). *John Thomas* is far less assertive. The lines dividing Sir Clifford, Nurse Bolton, and a worker like Bill Tewson

156   CLASS, POLITICS, AND THE INDIVIDUAL

are smudged. The two lovers are more inclined to escape both the "simmering and bubbling" energy of the workers, and the "frictional, seething, resistant, explosive, blind" energy of the owners (*JT*, 371). The fellowship that the first gamekeeper enjoyed, and Connie's relative security in joining her lover, are omitted in the second book. They have nowhere and no one to turn to. "It was exile, always exile," Connie says (*JT*, 373). And the final humiliation to them is delivered, ironically, by a worker, another gamekeeper. As Parkin and Connie take off their clothes in a deserted part of the woods surrounding the colliery, they are surprised and insulted by the new keeper. Rather than blame the squire who owns the woods, thereby making it impossible for the poor to enjoy their privacy, the worker complains that "yo' colliers, yo' all ower t' place!" (*JT*, 375). The social system just goes in circles—no progess is possible. "What's it matter! What's it matter! There's folks ivrywhere!" Parkin laments to Connie (*JT*, 375). Even nature, reminiscent of *Women in Love*, seems sterile: "The path, the whole hillside is a desert now, given over to rabbits and strolling colliers. In a sense it is dead. The kennels are grown deep in nettles. Dead as Ninevah!" (*JT*, 376). With this image the novel ends, not by looking toward the future, as did the *First Chatterley*, but by looking nostalgically to the past.

John Thomas and Lady Jane is significantly longer than either of the other two works. It has more characters. Certain ones like Sir Malcolm, Connie's father, and Hilda, her sister, are more fully developed. In many respects it is harder to pin down than either the first or third version because its characterizations and themes are more complex, and the characters and the major ideas are in greater conflict. The principal contradiction in *John Thomas* is between the major characters and their social setting. Connie and Parkin are genuinely horrified by capitalist industrialism and try to survive through each other, though ultimately they cannot escape an inherently socialized world. However complex Lawrence's notions were about change, he never fully accepted an absurdist notion of history—that neither social struggle nor society matters. Parkin's cry that "there's folks ivrywhere!" is one of despair, but it also acknowledges that other people do exist and must be acknowledged. At the end of *Women in Love*, everything seemed, to use Lawrence's word, so "inert": Gerald's body, the ice-covered mountains, and hope for the future. This cannot be said of *John Thomas*, a novel that maintains a balance among various uncertainties and contradictions without necessarily siding with any one

Radical Commitment to Eros   157

position. It contains curious disjunctions. Though, for example, his own station in life belies it, Clifford argues that "the proletariat is [. . .] a state of mind [. . .] not really a class at all" (*JT*, 293). Connie, for whom social class was everything, agrees, "There was no longer any such thing as class." This might have been one solution to the dilemma Lady Chatterley and Parkin find themselves in: caught between classes, loyal to none. By making class a fiction, a phenomenon so subjective that it hardly exists outside his heroes' imagination, Lawrence might have written a romantic bildungsroman, something like a sequel to *Sons and Lovers:* Paul Morel, alone after his mother's death, in despair over the cruelty of industrialism, war, and revolution, retreats into the security of a love affair.

Despite the appearance of subjectivity in *John Thomas*—like the utterances about the "disappearance" of class—no one is, in Georg Lukács's words, "strictly confined within the limits of his own experience." According to Lukács's definition of the "ideology of modernism," Lawrence's contemporaries, Kafka and Joyce, "compromised with the demands of historicity and of social environment." The hero in their works lacked "any pre-existent reality beyond his own self, acting upon him or being acted upon by him. Secondly, the hero himself is without personal history. He is 'thrown-into-the-world': meaninglessly, unfathomably."[1] Such a character can have no hope of changing his world; nor, in fact, does he himself usually undergo significant change. The vitality, however, of *John Thomas and Lady Jane* is that Lawrence avoids this stasis by continually showing the interrelatedness of class, individual psychology, and sexual relationships.

Thus does *John Thomas* move beyond *Women in Love* and *Lady Chatterley's Lover.* Despite Clifford and Connie's talk about the disappearance of class per se, the "polarised homogeneous proletariat" of "the human race," and Connie's hope that the "real phallic man" will rule the world, these illusions are continually shattered by the characters' own lives. In one instance, Connie begins to rhapsodize about some sailors she and her sister are watching. Connie is "overcome with the nostalgia of the old life, that is not nervous nor mechanical" (*JT*, 309). Her romanticized view of British class history is an echo of Lawrence's afterword, "A Propos of *Lady Chatterley's Lover*" (autumn 1929), where he refers to "the old England [when] the curious blood-connection held the classes together." Lady Chatterley, in version two, imagines that, as a lover, any one of these sailors would "be much nicer

158   Class, Politics, and the Individual

than our own sort." Hilda then reminds her that England is ruled by her class not by the transcendent spirit of the Wragby woods:

> These sailors are all just workmen, under somebody's authority. And Clifford and Everard and Duncan and Tommy are all in authority themselves. They are all masters, and these are just hired men. And a woman is always ashamed if she takes a hired man. She must take a master, somebody in authority, she can't submit to a man who is under another man. (*JT*, 310)

This is followed by an exchange that parodies the idealism of *Women in Love* and *Lady Chatterley's Lover*. In *John Thomas*, Connie tells Hilda that "there's something a bit starry" about her lover, the gamekeeper. "What is starry?" Hilda asks.

> "His body! even his penis! You don't know, Hilda, how strange it is, like a little god. Surely, surely it is more sacred than Clifford's being a baronet, or father's being an artist, or that awful Sir Andrew being so stinkingly rich. Surely it *really* means more—"
>
> "It may to you, at the moment. But even you'd get over it, and realize that Parkin's penis doesn't rule the world, whereas Clifford's baronetcy and Sir Andrew's money does,—father's art, too." (*JT*, 311)

In this passage, Connie's romanticism is brought up short. By contrast, her views are never seriously subject to rebuke in *Lady Chatterley's Lover*. An analogous passage in the third version that deals with the same theme—sexual intimacy as a socially subversive force—is never challenged. Lady Chatterley tells Mellors that "the courage of [his] own tenderness [. . .] will make the future." Mellors's reply is the novel's central message:

> Ay! It's tenderness, really; it's cunt-awareness. Sex is really only touch, the closest of all touch. And it's touch we're afraid of. We're only half-conscious, and half alive. We've got to come alive and aware. Especially the English have got to get into touch with one another a bit delicate and a bit tender. It's our crying need. (*LCL*, 301)

In *John Thomas*, by contrast, even Parkin's sexuality is derived from his working-class origins. His social roots are the source of his strength and his attractiveness to Lady Chatterley.

Compared to the third version, *John Thomas* is a more complex work for at least three reasons: it gives characters a life of their own apart from the omnipresent narrator of the third novel; it acknowl-

Radical Commitment to Eros 159

edges workers as a force distinct from the owners by continually reminding us that Parkin is a worker, despite Clifford's talk about class as a state of mind; it makes clear the impossibility of reintegrating the psyche and sexuality without resolving the larger class issue. Unlike the final version, in the second no farms exist to which Parkin may escape. Parkin tells Connie that factory work is "what other men has to [do]—pretty nigh every other man," so he must as well. "I'm a working-man, like a' th' rest" (*JT*, 351).

But as Lawrence neared *Lady Chatterley's Lover*, he stepped back from the political radicalism of the first novel. In *John Thomas*, Parkin is no longer a communist. "He is more or less of a socialist," Bill Tewson tells Connie. "But he is secretary for our club, an' he does have a bit of work screwing funds out of us boys" (*JT*, 356). Compared to *The First Lady Chatterley*, *John Thomas* hedges its politics. It is not nearly so confident that workers could be a force for social change. The novel is unambiguous on one point: class is an issue that must be reckoned with if modern man can reconstitute his relationships with women. In a letter to Dr. Trigant Burrow in 1927, Lawrence wrote that "it is our being cut off that is our ailment, and out of this ailment everything bad arises. [. . .] One has no real human relations—that is so devastating" (*CL*, 993). For all its twists and turns, *John Thomas and Lady Jane* ties together the question of class with the loss of personal intimacy.

Lady Chatterley's Lover: **In Retreat**

Lawrence completed *Lady Chatterley's Lover* in early January 1928. It was his last long work of fiction and, according to Rhys Davies, Lawrence said it was his "last large attempt to tell men and women how to live."[2] In this final version, Lawrence hoped to reconcile the social classes by muting the class "thing" and by emphasizing tenderness and reconciliation rather than social struggle. Within days of his completion of *Lady Chatterley*, Lawrence wrote the following letter to Rolf Gardiner, a letter that explains a great deal about his novel:

> The English are over-tender. They must have kindled again their religious sense of at-one-ness. And for that you must have a silent, central flame, a flame of *consciousness* and of warmth which radiates out bit by bit. Keep the core sound, and the rest will look after itself. What we need is reconciliation and atoning. (*CL*, 1031)

160   CLASS, POLITICS, AND THE INDIVIDUAL

But, as usual, Lawrence was simultaneously juggling a number of contending sentiments. Reconciliation could only come with attachment to people and to their struggles, but this was what gave Lawrence the most difficulty. He expressed his fear at "being so cut off." "I don't want to be," he wrote. "But anything else is either a personal tussle, or a money tussle: sickening. [. . .] One has no real human relations—that is so devastating" (*CL*, 993). Lawrence's correspondence during the months before and after January 1928 reflects the series of mental and physical crises he was undergoing. His health was rapidly deteriorating, and he felt his social isolation all the more bitterly. A British general strike had begun in May 1926, and a number of mining strikes had been broken by the Stanley Baldwin government.

Not surprisingly, Lawrence was caught in his old bind: wanting to defend the workers on strike, he was terrified of any solution involving militant class politics; he did not want a class war in England. In December 1928, nearly a year after *Lady Chatterley's Lover* was finished, Lawrence described in a rather broad way the kind of revolution he envisioned. Looking back on his novel, he commented on the plight of the striking miners:

> It's time there was an *enormous* revolution—not to install Soviets, but to give life itself a chance. What's the good of an industrial system piling up rubbish, while nobody lives. We want a revolution not in the name of money or work or any of that, but of life—and let money and work be as casual in human life as they are in a bird's life, damn it all. Oh it's time the whole thing was changed absolutely. And the men will have to do it—you've got to smash money and this beastly *possessive* spirit. I get more revolutionary every minute, but for *life's* sake. The dead materialism of Marx socialism and soviets seems to me no better than what we've got. What we want is life and trust; men trusting men, and making living a free thing, not a thing to be *earned*. But if men trusted men, we could soon have a new world, and send this one to the devil. (*CL*, 1110)

To accomplish these things—to give life a chance without socialism, soviets, and class struggle—Lawrence changed the characterization of Parkin. In addition, Lawrence used sexual intimacy as a way to subvert the status quo. He chose Mellors as his proponent of "the basic physical realities" because he owned no property, had no material aspirations, and his class identity was ambiguous. The gamekeeper had a mixed class background. He was the son of a blacksmith who worked in the mines. Mellors had been to

Radical Commitment to Eros 161

Sheffield Grammar School, became a junior clerk, and was an officer in India during World War I. He was more bourgeois than Parkin and had certain middle-class aspirations:

> [Mellors] seemed to Connie so unlike a gamekeeper, so unlike a working-man anyhow; although he had something in common with the local people. But also something very uncommon. "The gamekeeper, Mellors, is a curious kind of person," she said to Clifford; "he might almost be a gentleman." (*LCL*, 70)

For all these reasons, Mellors was the perfect character to "make an adjustment in consciousness to the basic physical realities."

By concentrating on the sexual motif to a far greater degree than in the earlier versions, Lawrence virtually guaranteed that his novel would end irresolutely, if not despairingly. In the first two works, social England is given a life of its own, beyond the occasional dismissal of classes by Clifford and his friends. In the scenes with Bill Tewson, his family, and Parkin, the reader can sense that, in Lawrence's words, "the working classes retain the old blood-warmth of oneness and togetherness" (*LCL*, 357). In *The First Lady Chatterley* and in *John Thomas*, bolshevik ideas were at least discussed. In *Lady Chatterley's Lover*, a great portion of historical England disappears. Instead of allowing an "essentially tragic age" to speak for itself, Lawrence magnified sexual relationships and minimize the conditions that gave rise to this tragic age. Often the novel is dominated by a narrator given to pronouncements, by a pedagogical Mellors, and by a relationship that is romanticized to the point that everyone and everything else in society is eclipsed. The rich tapestry of history, social struggle, and the interdependence of the public and private sectors is greatly diminished. Mellors relates to no one except Constance. The Tewson family is absent, and Mellors's penis is all but personified. Despite Lawrence's wish not to "go round, or scramble over the obstacles" of the social cataclysm, Mellors and Connie go out of their way to isolate themselves. The historical England of the first two versions now becomes largely two people, Wragby woods, the hut, and a few animals. Outsiders to these pastoral things are considered intruders, vulgar, or, like Clifford's crowd, ineffectual and effete.

The net effect of all this is to fog greatly Lawarence's view on society, class, politics, and the individual. Clearly this is not the same Lawrence who, while writing *The First Lady Chatterley*, stated in a letter to Dorothy Brett that his mood was "in a vile

162   CLASS, POLITICS, AND THE INDIVIDUAL

temper," one that "made me long for a bolshevist revolution which won't come" (*CL*, 961). *Lady Chatterley's Lover* reversed a theme he articulated in his 1926 short story, "The Man Who Loved Islands." This work satirized the notion that one can or should live apart from the social world. In the story, a man buys three islands and "presumes to fill [each one] with [his] own personality." The islands are, like Wragby woods are to Mellors and Connie, a place of refuge. What finally destroys the islander is not so much the violence force of physical nature but his alienation from any community or responsibility:

> The island was no longer a "world." It was a sort of refuge. The islander no longer struggled for anything. He had no need. It was as if he and his few dependents were a small flock of sea-birds alighted on this rock, as they travelled through space, and keeping together without a word. (*CS*, 734)

Before the appearance of *Lady Chatterley's Lover*, Lawrence had been expanding the scope of his characters' consciousness and attachments. Real tragedy, he wrote in a short story called "The Sun" (1925), "is lack of experience." In his essay called "Aristocracy," written during the summer of 1925, Lawrence wrote that "man is great according to his relation to the living universe is vast and vital" (*Ph* 2, 478). In 1928, when Lawrence completed *Lady Chatterley's Lover*, he wrote his "Autobiographical Sketch." Contrasted with his novel, this essay makes the novel even more an oddity. In this "Sketch," Lawrence self-critically took stock of his relationships with "my working people." The short essay is an agony of ambivalence, filled with the regrets of a "man from the working class" who cannot commit himself to people whose passion and "vibration" he finds "limited in another direction" from that of the middle class. The essay is replete with "but's" and "yet's." For all that, Lawrence comes to a positive though tentative resolution:

> Yet it is [workers], really, who form my *ambiente*, and it is from them that the human flow comes to me. I don't want to live with them in their cottages; that would be a sort of prison. But I want them to be there, about the place, their lives going on along with mine, and in relation to mine. I don't idealize them.[. . .] I don't expect them to make any millenium here on earth, either now nor in the future. But I want live near them, because their life still flows. [. . .]

Radical Commitment to Eros

163

> I cannot make the transfer from my own class into the middle class. I cannot, not for anything in the world, forfeit my passional consciousness and my blood-affinity with my fellow-men and the animals and the land, for that other thin, spurious mental conceit which is all that is left of the mental consciousness once it has made itself exclusive. (*Ph* 2,595)

Of all the ambivalences Lawrence articulated about himself and his work, this one was primary; unfortunately it is also the one most ignored by critics, despite the fact that the effects of Lawrence's troubled relationship to workers can be seen in all his works.

In an essay called "We Need One Another," published in May 1930, two months after his death, Lawrence directly attacked the sort of absolute individualism into which Mellors finally retreats. Throughout eleven novels, Lawrence had wrestled with the question of individual freedom and its limitations, the antagonistic pulls that private and communal concerns exert. Given the class nature of modern civilization, his novels ask, how could society best be reintegrated. In his essay "We Need One Another," Lawrence suggested that the efforts of Ursula, Birkin, Aaron, Lilly, Somers, and Mellors were at best heroic illusions. "In absolute isolation, I doubt if any individual amounts to much; or if any soul is worth saving, or even having," Lawrence wrote (*Ph 1*, 190). In "We Need One Another" he argued a dialectical view of history: the world's great heroes cannot be dissociated from the masses they represent and who organize themselves in behalf of such heroes:

> So that everything, even individuality itself, depends on relationship. "God cannot do without me," said an eighteenth-century Frenchman. What he meant was, that if there were no human beings, if Man did not exist, then God, the God of Man, would have no meaning. And it is true. If there were no men and women, Jesus would be meaningless. [. . .] The light does not shine with one half of the current. Every light is some sort of completed circuit. And so is every life, if it is going to be a life. (*Ph 1*, 190)

Much of the action in *Lady Chatterley's Lover* among the novel's three major spokesmen—Mellors, Tommy Dukes, and the narrator—tends to contradict this dominant trend in Lawrence's writings. Gone is the implicit acknowledgment of the first two versions that the reality upon which Wragby Hall depends is Tevershall; that whatever real passions are developed in the middle of the

164   CLASS, POLITICS, AND THE INDIVIDUAL

mechanization of industry and of the human spirit come from workers—from Parkin, Bill Tewson, and Nurse Bolton.

Lady Chatterley's Lover recalls, more than *John Thomas*, the way Birkin and Ursula handled the human blight caused by industrialism. For them a social-economic pathology required a very private solution. By the time Mellors and the narrator finish their declamations against society, which Mellors "knew by instinct to be a malevolent, partly-insane beast" (*LCL*, 127), both Wragby and Tevershall appear to be out for the third gamekeeper's blood. In the first two works, Lawrence had set up a dialectic between the strong working-class pronouncements of Parkin and Duncan against those of Sir Clifford. However, by *Chatterley* 3, Mellors and Connie see themselves set upon by "the malevolent Thing outside" the Wragby Woods, and this thing includes workers and owners alike. Nowhere but in *Lady Chatterley's Lover* can we read a description like that of Mellors, stalking around the Wragby Woods, looking for poachers and trying to make himself as invisible as possible to the surrounding collieries:

> Driven be desire and by the dread of the malevolent Thing outside, he made his round in the wood, slowly, softly. He loved the darkness and folded himself into it. [. . .] Oh, if only there were other men to be with, to fight that sparkling Thing outside there, to preserve the tenderness of life, the tenderness of women, and the natural riches of desire. If only there were men to fight side by side with! But the men were all outside there, glorying in the Thing, triumphing or being trodden down in the rush of mechanised greed or of greedy mechanism. (*LCL*, 127–28)

In *Lady Chatterley's Lover*, Lawrence switched his focus from the contradictions that a class society produced to a frame of reference that was more oriented toward sexual, intellectual, and psychic conflict. Although Wragby and Tevershall still exist, the issue in the final *Chatterley* version is not so much men exploiting men, but the modern mind lording it over the body. In the third version, Sir Clifford is as much a successful writer as he is a mine owner. His friends are less likely to be industrial bosses than writers: Charles May ("who wrote scientifically about stars"), Hamond, and Michaelis. "All were about the same age as Clifford; the young intellectuals of the day." These men, including Tommy Dukes, dismiss class struggle as "this hate business." Whereas the other Chatterley works discussed the relative merits of bolshevik ideol-

Radical Commitment to Eros

165

ogy, Lawrence now argues, through Dukes, that when the logical mind pretends to rule the roost, the roost turns into hate and "we're all Bolshevists, only we're hypocrites. The Russians are Bolshevists without hypocrisy" (*LCL*, 39).

The major characters—Sir Clifford, Nurse Bolton, Lady Chatterley, Tommy Dukes, Michaelis, Duncan Forbes, and Mellors—tend to agree on at least one point: the English are of one species, overly cerebral, sexually paralyzed, and socially apathetic, and all chasing the bitch-goddess of money. Nurse Bolton says the workers are "too decent" for bolshevism. "They only want a bit of money in their pocket, to spend at the Welfare, or go gadding to Sheffield. That's all they care" (*LCL*, 109). Connie then begins to deprecate workers:

> Connie thought, how extremely like all the rest of the classes the lower classes sounded. Just the same thing over again, Tevershall or Mayfair or Kensington. There was only one class nowadays: moneyboys. The moneyboy and the moneygirl, the only difference was how much you'd got, and how much you wanted. (*LCL, 110*)

What has gone bad in the world as pictured in this novel is not a social system per se but man's mental consciousness. Connie was filled with a "terror of the incipient insanity of the whole civilised species" (*LCL*, 116).

Apart from the obvious irony that the most cerebral of the three *Chatterley* novels has as one of its central themes "the swindle" of the mental life, the central characters arrive at an impasse that began in *John Thomas and Lady Jane* but that reaches its most despairing expression in the third work. Lawrence set out in the first version to describe the psychic and sexual dead-endedness of a society based upon class and exploitation. By *Lady Chatterley's Lover*, Lawrence felt that "the world was so complicated and weird and gruesome. The common people were so many, and really, so terrible (*LCL*, 171). The bosses were cold in their minds and bodies, and the industrial masses had "a life with utterly no beauty in it, no intuition, always 'in the pit.' " Real social subversiveness lies in our sexuality and one-to-one contact, not in the reordering of social relationships, but given the alignment of social forces in the novel, with Wragby and Tevershall positioned on either side of the woods, Mellors's sexual solution hardly seems plausible, in the final analysis, even to him. In fact, Lawrence's endorsement of Mellors is a qualified one. Most of the attention of the novel is

166   Class, Politics, and the Individual

focused on the gamekeeper, but as Lawrence presents him at the book's end, he is hardly a triumphant figure. One scene in particular illustrates Lawrence's conditional endorsement of his hero. In a dialogue between Mellors and Lady Chatterley, the gamekeeper presents his creed of warm-heartedness:

> "There's black days coming for us all and for everybody," he repeated with a prophetic gloom.
> "No! You're not to say it!"
> He was silent. [. . .] That was the death of all desire, the death of all love: this despair that was like the dark cave inside the men, in which their spirit was lost.
> "And you talk so coldly about sex," she said. "You talk as if you had only wanted your own pleasure and satisfaction. [. . .]
> "[. . .] you never believed in your women. You don't even believe really in me," she said.
> "I don't know what believing in a woman means."
> "That's it, you see! [. . .]
> "But what *do* you believe in?" she insisted.
> "I don't know."
> "Nothing, like all the men I've ever known," she said. [. . .]
> "Yes, I do believe in something. I believe in being warm-hearted. I believe especially in being warm-hearted in love, in fucking with a warm heart. I believe if men could fuck with warm hearts, and the women take warm-heartedly, everything would come all right. It's all this cold-hearted fucking that is death and idiocy." (*LCL*, 222)

This is not a dialogue between two people who have made their peace with the world; they are in flight from it. If their words prove anything, it is that in the absence of social ties, personal redemption is close to impossible.

In many respects *Lady Chatterley's Lover* is an experimental novel. The reasons for its thematic and stylistic departures from the first and second *Chatterley* are many. Fundamentally, however, the reason for its difference and the reason why it ultimately fails a a coherent and plausible statement about sex, the individual, and society is that Lawrence was unable to find an adequate solution to what ails everyone from Mellors to Sir Clifford. When Mellors tells Connie that he "doesn't believe in the world, not in money, nor in advancement, nor in the future of our civilisation," (*LCL*, 300), Lawrence sets the stage for the collapse of most of the prevailing ideas in the book; he almost guarantees they will not hold

Radical Commitment to Eros 167

up. In *The First Lady Chatterley*, the first sentence reads: "Ours is essentially a tragic age but we refuse emphatically to be tragic about it." In *John Thomas*, this beginning is expanded to:

> Ours is essentially a tragic age, so we refuse to take it tragically. The cataclysm has fallen, we've got used to the ruins, and we start to build up new little habitats, new little hopes. If we can't make a road through the obstacles, we go round, or climb over the top. (*JT*, 9)

Both these versions imply a certain hope for mankind, a certain willingness to go forward. However, in the third version, Lawrence changed the meaning, however subtly. "Ours is essentially a tragic age, so we refuse to take it tragically. The cataclysm has happened, we are among the ruins, we start to build up new little habitats, to have new little hopes" (*LCL*, 1). We may not go forward because now "we are among the ruins." Except when Mellors and Connie are making love, what is true for Sir Malcolm's family and Sir Clifford's is true for everyone: "It was talk that mattered supremely: the impassioned interchange of talk" (*LCL*, 3). Although Lawrence's portrayal of Sir Clifford is far from sympathetic, the mine owner's attitude toward his class, his father, the government, war, and people in general is similar to that of most of the characters: "In fact everything was a little ridiculous, or very ridiculous," the narrator tells us. Once such characters as Charlie May, Tommy Dukes, and Melleors blur the distinctions between capitalism and bolshevism, owner and worker, and between any and all ideas that may further social progress ("Hate's the inevitable outcome of forcing ideas on to life," says Dukes), a social cul-de-sac is inevitable.

Although the novel dimly acknowledges the power of workers by occasionally referring to the Bolshevik Revolution, revolution is faulted because social struggle is "all part of the life of the mine." In "A Propos of *Lady Chatterley's Lover*," Lawrence goes so far as to say that men's behavior *must* operate independently of the mind, that, in fact, "thought and action, word and deed, are two separate forms of consciousness, two separate lives which we lead" (*LCL*, 332). Worker and boss have been bolshevized, says Tommy Dukes, because we have forced ideas on to life. "We drive ourselves with a formula, like a machine. The logical mind pretends to rule the roost, and the roost turns into pure hate" (*LCL*, 39). In "A Propos," Lawrence takes this a step further: "But while we are in

168 CLASS, POLITICS, AND THE INDIVIDUAL

thought we cannot really act, and while we are in action we cannot really think. The two conditions, of thought and action, are mutually exclusive. Yet they should be raised in harmony" (*LCL*, 332). It is hard to imagine that the irony of this position escaped Lawrence: that through the interminable monologues of Mellors, Dukes, and the narrator, the reader could be led away from consciousness. One of the novel's central contradictions, which makes Mellors such a difficult character to accept, is that the gamekeeper who reads books on bolshevist Russia, travel, nuclear physics, geology, earthquakes, and India, and who upon occasion speaks like a Cambridge don, should advocate chucking mental consciousness for a phallic mystery. How does consciousness lead the mind away from itself?

To the extent that Lawrence identified with Mellors, he became increasingly bitter and contradictory. He was not happy with Mellor's role, and he seemed to be quarreling with himself. "The root of sanity is in the balls," Mellors tells Connie, not in trying to crank up the rusted motor car of society. Yet at the end of the book, in a long letter to Connie, Mellors is as much concerned with the apathy of the British working class as he is with his desire to fan the flames of sexuality. The workers "grumble a lot," he writes, "but they're not going to alter anything." Earlier Lawrence had argued, through Dukes, that "each man is a machine-part, and the driving power of the machine, hate [. . .] hate of the bourgeois. That to me, is Bolshevism" (*LCL*, 38). Bolshevism is another form of the paralysis that emanates from the mind. Now, in his farewell letter, Mellors rues that "the men are very apathetic" and ill-prepared to take any sort of social *action:*

> They feel the whole damned thing is doomed, and I believe it is. And they are doomed along with it. Some of the young ones spout about a Soviet but there's not much conviction in them. There's no sort of conviction about anything, except that it's all a muddle and a hole. (*LCL*, 325)

Until the last line, Lawrence argued with himself as to the importance of social struggle, its limitations, and the potential for physical tenderness to heal society's wounds. Mellors may have the last word, but his is hardly a triumphant position. He and Lady Chatterley are apart; the "little forked flame" between the lovers is just that—little, barely warming anyone. Both Mellors and his John Thomas are "a little drooping."

Radical Commitment to Eros

The *Chatterley* Trilogy

Lady Chatterley's Lover is best viewed in the wider context of the three versions, wherein the last work appears as a more developed and complicated expression of themes inchoate in the first two. The themes of flawed sexuality, the failure of modern consciousness to effect change, the irrelevance of class struggle, and the regenerating potential of genital power can be found in the three *Chatterley* novels. So can a counter notion that social and economic relationships, as much as sexuality, determine our destinies. Lawrence was experimenting with disparate ideas, trying them out. No one of these ever thoroughly dominated the *Chatterley* trilogy.

The three works, like Lawrence's novels as a whole, clearly elude an overall design or cohesive pattern. Lawrence believed this was the only way his craft could stay alive. In an essay called "Why the Novel Matters" (1925), Lawrence argued that for an author to grow in any one direction would as soon kill the novel as pouring salt on the roots of a plant. His essay is a plea for the integrity of experimentation of ideas and the author's willingness to let his characters go. "A character in a novel has got to live," Lawrence wrote, "or it is nothing" (*Ph* 1, 537). Lawrence was not after a system of ideas but the free exchange of them:

> I don't want to grow in any one direction any more. And, if I can help, I don't want to stimulate anybody else into some particular direction. A particular direction ends in a *cul-de-sac*. We're in a *cul-de-sac* at present. [. . .]
> We should ask for no absolutes or absolute. Once and for all and for ever, let us have done with the ugly imperialism of any absolute. There is no absolute good, there is nothing absolutely right. All things flow and change, and even change is not absolute. The whole is a strange assembly of apparently incongruous parts, slipping past one another. (*Ph 1*, 536)

In different ways, every one of the *Chatterley* novels attacks the psychic, sexual, and social imperialism of the historical period. The underlying tensions in his works are caused by the shifting value Lawrence attached to the private and public character of men and women: Which precedes the other? How important is class? What priority should be given to the individual? Is change effected primarily through social or private means? Perhaps, above all else, Lawrence hated the imposition of society or of individuals upon

170 CLASS, POLITICS, AND THE INDIVIDUAL

others—"the ugly imperialism of any absolute." Lawrence's mistrust of any absolute explains why his *Chatterley* works keep opening up new territory, raising new questions, and why they often contradict one another. "Only in the novel," Lawrence wrote in "Why the Novel Matters," "Are *all* things given full play, or at least, they may be given full play, when we realize that life itself, and not inert safety, is the reason for living" (*Ph 1*, 538). Safety and inertness are qualities not found in the *Lady Chatterley* novels.

Notes

1. Georg Lukács, *The Meaning of Contemporary Realism*, trans. John Mander and Necke Mander (London: Merlin Press, 1963), p. 21.

2. Edward Nehls, ed., *D. H. Lawrence: A Composite Biography*, 3 vols., vol. 2 (Madison: University of Wisconsin Press, 1959), p. 274.

Bibliography

Aldington, Richard. *D. H. Lawrence: Portrait of a Genius But. . . .* New York: Collier, 1950.

Avineri, Shlomo. *The Social and Political Thought of Karl Marx.* Cambridge: Cambridge University Press, 1969.

Beal, Anthony. *D. H. Lawrence.* New York: Grove Press, 1961.

Becker, George. *D. H. Lawrence.* New York: Frederick Ungar, 1980.

Booth, Wayne. "Objectivity in Fiction." In *Twentieth-Century Literary Criticism.* Edited by David Lodge. London: Longman, 1972.

Boulton, James T., ed. *The Letters of D. H. Lawrence.* Vol. 1. September 1901–May 1913. Cambridge: Cambridge University Press, 1979.

Caudwell, Christopher. *Studies and Further Studies in a Dying Culture.* New York: Monthly Review Press, 1971.

Cavitch, David. *D. H. Lawrence and the New World.* New York: Oxford University Press, 1969.

Cole, G. D. H. *A Short History of the British Working Class Movement, 1789–1947.* Rev. ed. London: George Allen and Unwin, 1948.

Cowan, James C. *D. H. Lawrence's American Journey: A Study in Literature and Myth.* Cleveland: The Press of Case Western Reserve University, 1970.

Daleski, H. M. "The Tiger and the Lamb: The Quality of Lawrence." In *Critics on D. H. Lawrence,* edited by W. T. Andrews. Coral Gables: University of Miami Press, 1971.

Eagleton, Terry. *Exiles and Emigrés: Studies in Modern Literature.* New York: Schocken, 1970.

Ford, George H. *Double Measure: A Study of the Novels and Stories of D. H. Lawrence.* New York: Holt, Rinehart and Winston, 1965.

Freeman, Mary. *D. H. Lawrence: A Basic Study of His Ideas.* New York: Universal Library, Grosset and Dunlop, 1955.

Harrison, John. *The Reactionaries: A Study of the Anti-Democratic Intelligentsia.* New York: Schocken, 1967.

Hochman, Baruch. *Another Ego: The Changing View of Self and Society*

172 CLASS, POLITICS, AND THE INDIVIDUAL

in the Works of D. H. Lawrence. Columbia: University of South Carolina Press, 1970.

Hough, Graham. *The Dark Sun.* New York: Capricorn, 1956.

Jerrett-Kerr, Martin. *D. H. Lawrence and Human Existence.* London: SCM Press, 1961.

Kazin, Alfred. "Sons, Lovers, and Mothers." In *Sons and Lovers,* edited by Julian Moynahan. New York: Viking Press, 1968.

Kermode, Frank. *D. H. Lawrence.* New York: Viking Press, 1973.

Kessler, Jascha. "The Myth of *The Plumed Serpent.*" In *A D. H. Lawrence Miscellany,* edited by Harry T. Moore. Carbondale: Southern Illinois University Press, 1959.

Kettle, Arnold. *An Introduction to the English Novel.* Vol. 2. New York: Harper and Brothers, 1960.

Lawrence, Frieda. "D. H. Lawrence, the Failure." In *D. H. Lawrence: A Collection of Criticisms,* edited by Leo Hamalian. New York: McGraw-Hill, 1973.

Leavis, F. R. *D. H. Lawrence: Novelist.* New York: Simon and Schuster, 1968.

Lukács, Georg. *The Meaning of Contemporary Realism.* Translated by John Mander and Necke Mander. London: Merlin Press, 1963.

McKHenry, G. B. "Carrying On: *Lady Chatterley's Lover.*" In *Critics on D. H. Lawrence,* edited by W. T. Andrews. Coral Gables: University of Miami Press, 1971.

Miko, Stephen. *Toward* Women in Love: *The Emergence of a Lawrentian Aesthetic.* New Haven: Yale University Press, 1971.

Moore, Harry T. *The Life and Works of D. H. Lawrence.* New York: Twayne, 1951.

Morton, A. L. *A People's History of England.* London: Lawrence and Wishart, 1945.

Moynahan, Julian. "*Sons and Lovers:* The Search for Form." In *Sons and Lovers,* edited by Julian Moynahan. New York: Viking Press, 1968.

Mudrick, Marvin. "The Originality of *The Rainbow.*" In *A D. H. Lawrence Miscellany,* edited by Harry T. Moore. Carbondale: Southern Illinois University Press, 1959.

Murray, John Middleton. "Genius and a Syndrome." In *Sons and Lovers,* edited by Julian Moynahan. New York: Viking Press, 1968.

————. *Son of Woman: The Story of D. H. Lawrence.* New York: Jonathan Cape and Harrison Smith, 1931.

Nehls, Edward, ed. *D. H. Lawrence: A Composite Biography.* Vol. 2. Madison: University of Wisconsin Press, 1959.

Pinion, F. B. *A D. H. Lawrence Companion.* New York: Harper and Row, 1979.

Bibliography 173

Pinto, Vivian de Sola. "D. H. Lawrence." In *The Politics of Twentieth-Century Novelists,* edited by G. A. Panichas. New York: Thomas Y. Crowell, 1974.

Pritchard, R. E. *D. H. Lawrence: Body of Darkness.* London: Hutchinson, 1971.

Sagar, Keith. *The Art of D. H. Lawrence.* Cambridge: Cambridge University Press, 1966.

Sanders, Scott. *D. H. Lawrence: The World of the Five Major Novels.* New York: Viking Press, 1973.

Schorer, Mark. "*Women in Love* and Death." In *D. H. Lawrence: A Collection of Critical Essays,* edited by Mark Spilka. Englewood Cliffs, N.J.: Prentice-Hall, 1963.

Shaw, George Bernard. "Introduction to *Hard Times.*" In *Hard Times,* edited by George Ford and Sylvere Monod. New York: W. W. Norton, 1966.

Spender, Stephen. *The Destructive Element: A Study of Modern Writers and Beliefs.* Philadelphia: Albert Saifer, 1963.

Stoll, John. *The Novels of D. H. Lawrence: A Search for Integration.* Columbia: University of Missouri Press, 1971.

Strachey, John. *Literature and Dialectical Materialism.* New York: Covici, Friede, 1934.

Tindall, William York. *Forces in Modern British Literature: 1885–1956.* New York: Vintage, 1956.

Van Ghent, Dorothy. *The English Novel: Form and Function.* New York: Holt, Rinehart and Winston, 1953.

Vivas, Eliseo. *D. H. Lawrence: The Failure and the Triumph of Art.* Bloomington: Indiana University Press, 1960.

Waterman, Arthur. "The Plays of D. H. Lawrence." In *D. H. Lawrence: A Collection of Critical Essays,* Mark Spilka. Englewood Cliffs, N.J.: Prentice-Hall, 1963.

Williams, Raymond. *Culture and Society, 1780–1950.* London: Chatto and Windus, 1960.

———. *The English Novel from Dickens to Lawrence.* New York: Oxford University Press, 1973.

———. *Modern Tragedy.* Stanford: Stanford University Press, 1965.

Worthen, John. *D. H. Lawrence and the Idea of the Novel.* Totowa: Rowman and Littlefield, 1979.

Young, Kenneth. *D. H. Lawrence.* Published for the British Council and the National Book League by Longmans, Green, 1952.

Yudishtar. "The Changing Scene: *Aaron's Rod.*" In *D. H. Lawrence: A Collection of Criticism,* edited by Leo Hamalian. New York: McGraw-Hill, 1973.

Index

Aaron's Rod, 17–18, 39, 42–43, 60, 67–68, 77, 84–85, 89–90, 92–111, 114, 118, 122, 127, 134–36, 138, 140–41
"A Propos of *Lady Chatterley's Lover*," 157, 167–68
Apocalypse, 135
"Aristocracy," 162
Aristocracy, aristocrats, 14–16, 43–46, 65–66, 77, 82–84, 90, 92, 94, 103–6, 110, 113, 119–20, 148, 150, 152. *See also* Democracy; Middle Class
Asquith, Lady Cynthia, 65, 87
"Autobiographical Fragment," 24, 76, 139
"Autobiographical Sketch," 9, 24–26, 53, 162–63

Baldwin, Stanley: government of, 160
Becker, George, 88
Bourgeois. *See* Middle class
Brett, Dorothy, 161
Brewster, Earl H., 92, 140–41, 145
British General Strike, 70, 138, 160
British Morality Council, 52
Burrow, Dr. Trigant, 143–44
Bynner, Witter, 146

Campbell, Gordon, 13, 41
Cannan, Mary, 12, 43
Chartists, 70
Class, theme of, 9, 10, 12–13, 18–20, 23–24, 26–27, 36, 38, 42, 54, 56, 71–74, 77, 84–85, 98, 116, 126, 134, 137, 145, 152, 156, 161, 165, 169. *See also* Lawrence, David Herbert: class as a theme
Cole, G. D. H., 44–45, 69
Collier's Friday Night, A, 70–74, 76
Collings, Ernest, 41

Communism, Communist Party, 14, 43, 70, 84, 89, 109, 148–49, 152, 159. *See also* Socialism, Socialists

"Daughter-in-Law, The," 70
David, 72
Davies, Rhys, 159
"Death of a Porcupine," 119, 136
"Democracy," 95, 111–13
Democracy, 13–16, 44–46, 60, 65, 83–84, 94, 98, 109, 111–13, 115–16, 124, 143, 148–49. *See also* Aristocracy, aristocrats; Fascism; Race, racism
Dickens, Charles, 82–83
Dostoyevsky, Feodor, 119

"Education of the People," 95, 146–47

Fantasia of the Unconscious, 89–91, 134
Fascism, fascists, 78, 89–90, 94–95, 98, 103, 109–11, 113, 118, 124, 134, 141–42, 152
First Lady Chatterley, The, 19, 23, 83, 134, 137–38, 140, 142, 144–56, 159, 161, 167
Frank, Waldo, 59
Freeman, Mary, 94
French Revolution, 15

Gardiner, Rolf, 94, 138–39, 142–43, 150, 159–60
Garnett, Constance, 57
Garnett, Edward, 40
Graham, R. B. Cunninghame: *Pedro de Valdivia,* 146
"Grand Inquisitor, The," 119

Hard Times (Dickens), 83
Harrison, John, 94

Index

175

Industrialism, 10, 12, 19, 27–29, 34–35, 37–38, 46–51, 55–56, 59–60, 63, 66, 73–76, 79, 86, 91, 94, 140, 143, 151–52, 156–57, 160, 164–65

"Introduction to *Memoirs of the Foreign Legion*," 111, 114

John Thomas and Lady Jane, 137, 146, 151–59, 161, 163–65, 167
Joyce, James, 115, 157

Kafka, Franz, 157
Kangaroo, 17, 39, 46, 60, 68, 77–78, 84, 89–90, 100, 109, 111, 113–27, 134–36, 138, 141, 150
Koteliansky, S. S., 138–39

Lady Chatterley: three versions of, 12, 23, 40, 60, 137–40, 143–48, 153–70
Lady Chatterley's Lover, 13, 18, 23, 84–85, 115, 145, 147, 155, 157–70
Lawrence, David Herbert: class as a theme, 9–10, 12–13, 18–20, 23–24, 26–27, 36, 38, 42, 54, 56, 71–74, 77, 82, 84–85, 98, 116, 126, 134, 137, 145, 152, 156, 161, 165, 169; mystical qualities, 12, 33, 49–50, 56, 61, 68–69, 113, 118, 121, 124, 126, 128, 132–34, 149; political positions, 10–11, 27, 37, 42, 47, 58, 65, 77, 82, 84–87, 89, 91–93, 98–99, 103, 107, 111–13, 120, 123–24, 129, 132–33, 136, 144, 147, 152, 156, 160; view of art and artists, 19, 41, 86, 98, 100–101, 106, 111, 115, 124–25, 144; view of the novel, 41, 100, 115, 124–25, 144, 170; view of revolution, 11–19, 42–43, 53, 58, 77–78, 83–85, 87, 97, 99, 114–15, 127, 139, 142, 144, 148, 157, 160, 162, 167
Lawrence, Frieda, 14, 17, 131
Lloyd George, David, 71, 99
Lost Girl, The, 17, 84, 122, 141, 147
Luhan, Mable Dodge 137, 141, 150
Lukács, Georg, 93, 157, 170n

"Man Who Loved Islands, The," 150
Manfield, Katherine, 58
Meacham, Standish, 44
Melville, Herman, 133
"Merry-Go-Round, The," 70
Middle class, 9–10, 16, 24–26, 31–33, 36, 53, 60, 62–64, 69, 73–74, 76–77, 96, 104–5,

133, 143, 148, 152–53, 161–63, 168
"Miner at Home, The," 76
"Morality and the Novel," 101
Morrell, Lady Ottoline, 14–15, 42–44, 53, 58–59, 87
Morton, A. L., 70–71, 87n, 88n
Movements in European History, 83, 91, 101
Myth, 13, 94, 125–27, 132–33

Nature, 10, 27–28, 38–39, 47–50, 122–23
Nehls, Edward, 170n
"Nottingham and the Mining Countryside," 27, 76
"Novel, The," 144

"Odour of Chrysanthemums," 75

Pansies: "Saddest Day, The," 9; "Prestige," 25; "Climbing Up," 31–32
Pedro de Valdivia (Cunninghame Graham), 146
Plumed Serpent, 12, 60, 77–78, 89–90, 92–94, 98, 100, 109, 111, 115, 119, 123–36, 138, 142, 145, 147, 150
Politics, 10–11, 27, 37, 42, 47, 58, 65, 77, 82, 84–87, 89, 91–93, 98–99, 103, 107, 111–13, 120, 123–24, 129, 132–33, 136, 144, 147, 152, 156, 160. *See also* Revolution; Russian Revolution

Race, racism, 78, 94, 100, 102, 128–32
Rainbow: as a symbol, 46, 50, 52–53, 56
Rainbow, The, 10, 12, 15–17, 23, 26, 39–57, 61, 68–69, 85, 91–96, 122, 133–34, 147, 151
Reactionaries, The (Harrison), 94
"Reality of Peace, The," 95
Reflection on the Death of a Porcupine, 78, 94, 109
Revolution, 11–19, 42–43, 53, 58, 77–78, 83–85, 87, 97, 99, 114–15, 127, 139, 142, 144, 148, 157, 160, 162, 167
Right to Work Bill, 45
Russell, Bertrand, 11, 15–16, 44, 45–46, 65, 87
Russian Revolution, 13, 57–58, 71, 83, 148, 162, 164–65, 168. *See also* Revolution

Sanders, Scott, 13, 20n
Sex, sexual instinct and intimacy, 12–13, 19,

176   CLASS, POLITICS, AND THE INDIVIDUAL

24, 26–27, 29, 33–34, 42, 46, 64, 68, 75, 102, 134, 144, 147, 150, 154, 157–61, 164–66, 168–69
Shaw, George Bernard, 83, 88n.
Sisters, The, 40
Socialism, socialists, 80, 89–92, 95, 98, 103, 111–12, 124, 126, 129, 132–34, 141, 160. *See also* Communism: Fascism
Sons and Lovers, 10, 12, 23–24, 26–40, 70, 72, 74, 85, 91, 101, 110, 122, 157
"State of Funk, The," 145
"Strike," 76
Studies in Classic American Literature, 19, 86
"Surgery for the Novel—Or a Bomb," 111, 115

Tenderness, 115, 140, 149

Touch and Go, 73, 76–87
Triple Alliance, 71

War, 13–15, 18, 42, 44–45, 52, 56, 58–59, 71, 89, 90–91, 95, 97, 101, 110, 114, 116, 146, 148–49, 157. *See also* Revolution
Wedding Ring, The, 40
"We Need Each Other," 163
"Why the Novel Matters," 169–70
Widowing of Mrs. Holroyd, The, 70–76
"Woman Who Rode Away, The," 141
Women in Love, 17–18, 23, 27, 31, 39, 46, 53, 56–69, 77, 79, 81, 84–85, 87, 91, 95–96, 122–23, 129, 134, 141, 147, 151–53, 156
World War I, 12–13, 45, 56, 70–71, 92, 95–96, 107, 109, 115, 139, 161